W9-AWO-901

Popular Mechanics

The Boy Magician

Popular Mechanics

THE BOY MAGICIAN

156 AMAZING TRICKS *and* SLEIGHTS *of* HAND

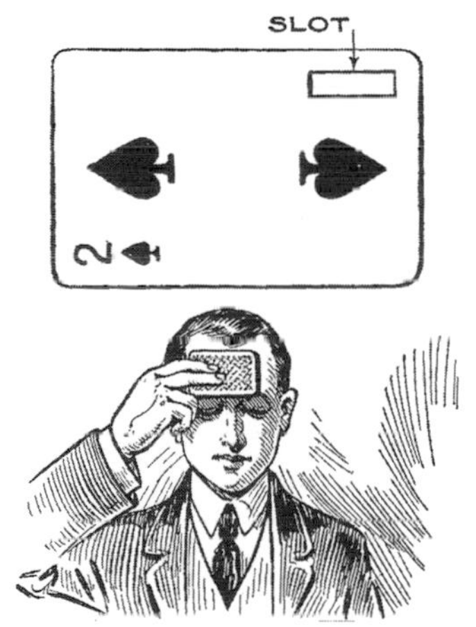

HEARST BOOKS
A division of Sterling Publishing Co., Inc.

New York / London
www.sterlingpublishing.com

Contents

PERFECT PARTY TRICKS

BIG-ACT CROWD PLEASERS

CHANGE CHANGE

Popular Mechanics

The Boy Magician

Foreword

It's a wonderful place, this world of magic—where flowers appear instantaneously, coins vanish into thin air, skeletons can be made to dance, and reality is suspended, if only for few moments. Just about any young magician will be able to master the 156 tricks in this book—whether simple ones like the floating hat, or more complex illusions such as the goldfish that travels from bowl to bowl. The beauty of the magic presented here is that it is no less impressive for its ease of execution. And from the moment an ordinary boy learns his first simple card trick, or how to palm a coin, he is transformed into that most exciting of characters—the magician.

Building a repertoire is the goal of any self-respecting magician, so for those who have mastered the basics such as having a chosen card levitate out of the deck, there are more complex magical challenges such as pulling thirty-six cannonballs out of a small bag, making "spirits" play the violin, or even creating a magic cave from which to conjure just about anything from an apple to a glass vase. We've also included tricks that rely on that mysterious gap between hand and eye—the power of illusion—and we offer an entire section covering the magic of science, which will easily be the most fun any student will have while learning. Plus there are projects for special equipment the magician can make to enhance the performance.

So the budding magician need never stop at a few simple card tricks.

Take those tricks and add a handkerchief that collects candies from midair, a borrowed watch that seems to bend as if it were made of rubber, and the mystery of the "magic candles," and now he's got a riveting performance suitable for friends and family. It's only for the young magician to plumb the depths of this book and the audience will always be left amazed, impressed, and wanting more.

The Editors of
Popular Mechanics

{CHAPTER 1}

CARD SHARK

Deck Dexterity

— Forcing the Card —

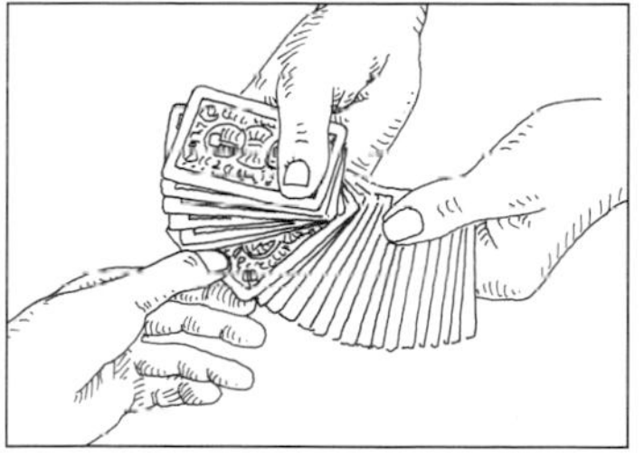

Although not a trick itself, this subtle and useful sleight of hand is essential for the performance of many other card tricks. It requires only a bit of skill, but the magician needs to be confident of the maneuver for it to work. In offering the fan of cards from which a volunteer is to select one, an individual card is pushed forward. The magician should take pains to look directly at the volunteer, subtly shifting the deck so that the card to be chosen is only slightly exposed more than those around it.

In the event that the card chosen is not the card to be forced, the magician says, "I see the card you've chosen is damaged, so in the interest of fairness, you should take another."

— The Basic Card Pick —

Spread the pack, like a fan, toward some member of your audience and ask him to choose a card. Have a card freely chosen and taken from the pack unseen by the others. Then hand the pack out to be shuffled. When you have received the pack again, spread it out fan-wise, as it was previously. Ask your volunteer to insert his card—which he has noted—in any part of the pack he likes. As he is doing this, your forefinger of the right hand, which is naturally under the cards, comes forward and meets the chosen card. The instant you feel it, press the fingernail into the edge of the card, thus making a slight indentation. This will be quite unnoticed by anyone but you. The mark must be made very lightly. The pack may be shuffled again, and when you have gone through it carefully, the chosen card may be picked out with little difficulty.

— The "X-Ray" Pack of Cards —

This trick is a "mind-reading" stunt that is worked on a new principle, and it is very puzzling. A full pack of cards is shown and half of them are handed out, the other half being kept by the performer. A spectator is asked to select any card from those he has been given, then insert it in the pack held by the performer, while the latter's eyes are closed or his head is turned. Without manipulating the pack in any way, the performer places it against his forehead and instantly names the card chosen by the spectator.

In advance, the performer prepares the pack he is going to hold for the trick by cutting a slot ⅛ in. wide and 1 in. long in one corner of twenty-five cards, using the sharp point of a penknife, in such a manner that all the slots coincide. In presenting the trick, the performer keeps all the prepared cards—and one card that has no slot, the latter being kept on top of the pack so that the spectators cannot see the slots. The performer's thumb is held over the slots when the bottom of the pack is shown. The spectator is asked to insert a card face down into the cards the performer holds in his hand. When this is done, the performer lifts his thumb from the slot as the cards are raised to the forehead, so that he can look through the pack and see the index (identifying the number and suit) on the card the spectator has selected. After the forehead "stall," the performer announces the card selected. The trick is repeated by "fanning" out the cards and extracting the card named.

— The False Shuffle —

The effect of any card trick may be greatly enhanced by shuffling the pack, after having noticed (secretly, of course) the bottom card. This apparently does away with any previous arrangement. The object of the shuffle is to leave the pack, or certain cards in it, in exactly the same position they were in before. Shuffles of this kind, which leave certain cards undisturbed, are known as "false shuffles." There are many ingenious methods for shuffling the pack in this manner. For our present purposes, here are just two of the methods that leave the bottom card still at the bottom, or the top card at the top.

One method of affecting this is as follows: Take the pack in the left hand in the ordinary way and then shuffle it with the right, leaving a number of cards alternately at the front and rear of the pack. That is, leave some at the top, then some at the bottom, some more at the top, and so on. Take care that the last batch shall always be at the bottom of the pack. This leaves the bottom card always in its original place.

Here's another method: Divide the pack equally into two packets, seeing that the card known to you is on the bottom of one of these packets, and noting which one. Now lift the corners of the two packets and let the cards fall alternately as nearly as possible, the corners overlapping so that when the shuffle is finished, the two packets form one entire pack. The only thing you have to attend to here is to see that the card known to you falls onto the table first. This leaves that particular card still at the bottom of the pack. This method may also be employed for keeping in sight the top card (in which case, of course, this card falls last).

— Magically Naming a Written Card —

This experiment consists of requesting anyone in a group of spectators to name a card and write it on a piece of paper, whereupon the performer instantly names the card written.

Two people are needed for the trick, the performer and his assistant. The performer leaves the room while the spectator writes the name of the card on the paper, with the assistant supplying the paper and pencil—and observing what's being written. After the name of the card is written, the spectator folds the paper and hands it to the assistant along with the pencil. The assistant lays the pencil and paper on a table in certain positions that are prearranged to designate the name of the card. Previous to this trick, the performer and the assistant must have the positions of the paper and pencil mentally fixed in their minds. Referring to the sketch, the four sides of the table represent the card suits: spades, hearts, clubs, and diamonds. An imaginary circle divided into twelve parts (like a clock dial) indicates the number of the

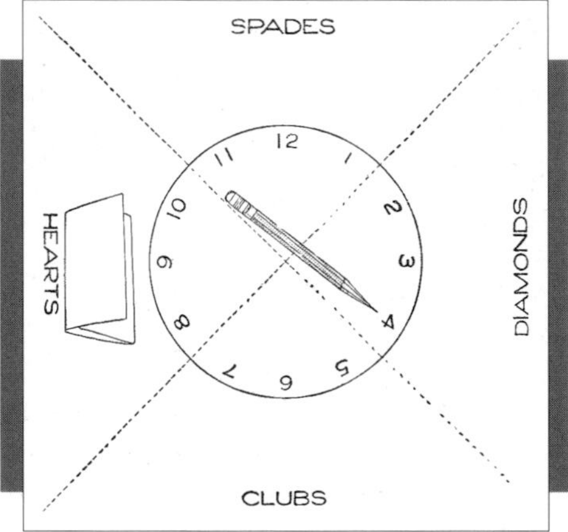

The markings are memorized, so that only the positions of the pencil and paper will be seen.

card, with 1 standing for ace, 2 for deuce, and so on.

The assistant, knowing what has been written on the paper, lays it on one side of the table to indicate the suit. The pencil is placed so that it points to the number on the imaginary circle or dial. The one shown in the sketch is designating the four of hearts.

— Mechanical Trick with Cards —

The following mechanical card trick is easy to prepare and simple to perform: First, procure a new deck and divide it into two piles, one containing the red cards and the other the black ones, all cards facing the same way. Take the red cards, square them up, and place them in a vise. Then use a plane to shave about 1/16 in. off the upper right-hand corner and lower left-hand corner, as in *Figure 1.*

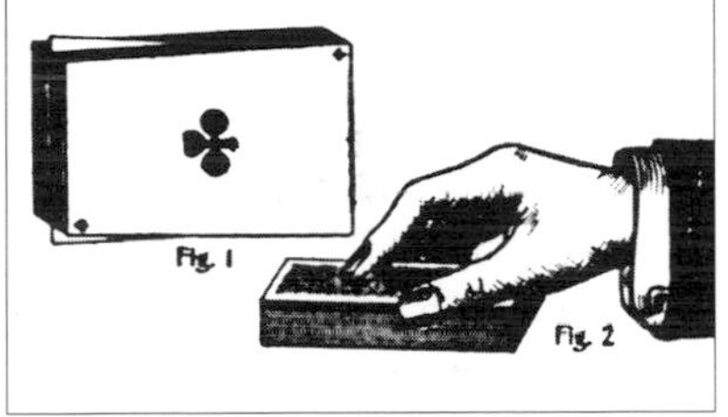

The Shaved Cards

Then take the black cards, square them up, and plane off about 1/16 in. at the upper left-hand and lower right-hand corners.

Next, restore all the cards to one pack. Take care to make the first card red, the next black, and so on, so that every alternate card is the same color. Bend the pack so as to give some spring to the cards. If you hold one thumb on the upper left-hand corner, all the cards will appear red to the audience. Place your thumb in the top center of the pack (*Figure 2)*, and they will appear mixed, red and black. With a thumb on the upper right-hand corner, all cards will appear black. You can therefore display either color called for.

— Two Effective Card Tricks —

The first trick involves the use of four cards, which are "fanned" out, to show a corresponding number of kings. The performer repeats the magical word "abracadabra"—and presto! The same hand has changed to four aces when it is again displayed. After another pass, only blank cards are shown.

Six cards are required for this trick, three of which are unprepared, the other three "prepared." The three unprepared cards are the king and ace of spades as well as a blank card, as shown in *Figure 1.* The three other cards—the other aces—are prepared by pasting a portion of the remaining three kings over a corner of the aces of their corresponding suits, as shown in *Figure 2.* In addition, the index (showing an ace and the suit) in a corner of the aces should be erased or covered up; otherwise, it will be impossible to show the "blank cards" later.

In the presentation of this trick, the "four kings" are first displayed to the audience. With the real king on the top, the cards are fanned as in *Figure 3,* so as to show only the pasted king on the corner of each of the other three cards. Then the performer picks up the unprepared ace of spades, which has been left face up on the table. He announces that he will place it directly behind the king of spades, which he does. He then lays the king of spades (the unprepared king) on the table. The cards are then closed up and turned over so that they are now being held at what was the top of the cards in the first presentation, of the four kings. This time the cards are fanned out to show the four aces, as in *Figure 4.*

The manipulator now states that by placing a blank card (which he picks up from the table) where the ace of spades is, he will make the spots disappear from all of the cards. The ace of spades is placed on the table, with the blank card taking its place. The cards are then closed and fanned out again, this time with the hand showing four blank cards, as in *Figure 5.*

In the second trick, an ace of diamonds is held in one hand and an ace of spades in the other. Although both are held in full view of the audience, the cards change places.

The prepared cards are made from two aces of diamonds, from which the corner index pips (the diamond shapes) and letters have been erased. An ace of spades is also required, the center of which is cut from the rest of the card as indicated in *Figure 6,* which shows the appearance of the three prepared cards. In presenting this particular trick, an ace of diamonds is held in each hand, but only one of them is visible to the audience; the other is concealed

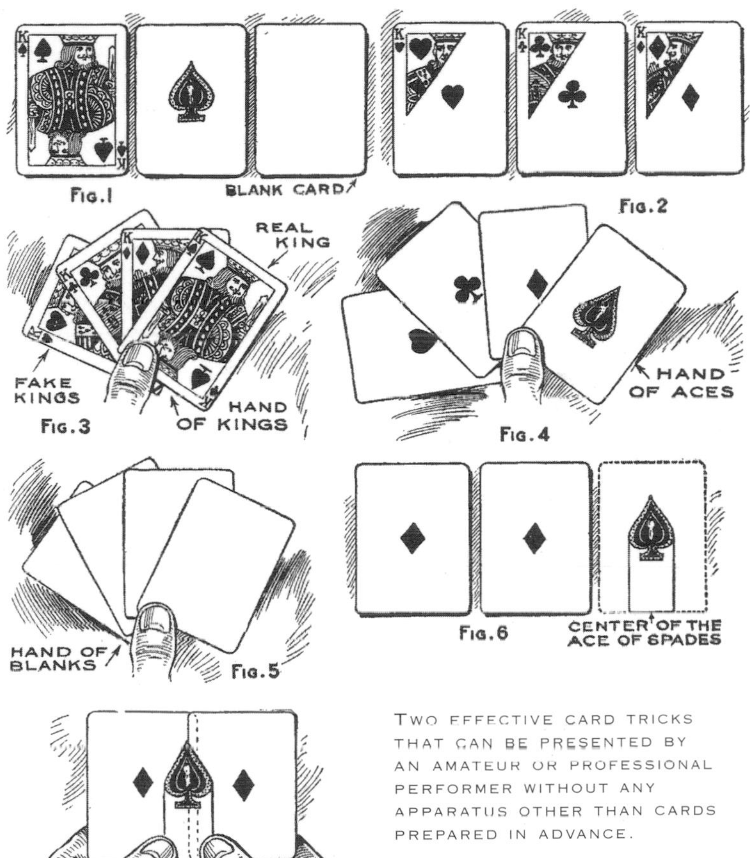

TWO EFFECTIVE CARD TRICKS THAT CAN BE PRESENTED BY AN AMATEUR OR PROFESSIONAL PERFORMER WITHOUT ANY APPARATUS OTHER THAN CARDS PREPARED IN ADVANCE.

underneath the ace that has been cut from the card. The performer then announces his intention of making the cards change places.

He turns the backs of the cards toward the audience and, with his hands apart, begins moving the cards back and forth, bringing them a little closer to each other at each pass. Finally, when the edges touch, as in *Figure 7*, the false center from the card is slipped over and onto the other card. This done, the cards are again moved back and forth, gradually separating them, and their faces are once more turned to the audience. To all appearances, the cards have changed positions.

— Mind-Reading Effect with Cards —

Five cards are shown, and one person is asked to think of two cards in the lot. After this, the performer places the cards behind his back and removes any two cards, then shows the remaining three and asks if the two cards in mind have been removed. The answer is always yes, as it cannot be otherwise.

To prepare the cards, take any ten cards from the pack and paste the back of one card to another, making five double cards. Removing any two cards behind the performer's back reduces the number of cards to three, and when these are shown—turned over to the other side—they will not have the same faces; therefore, the ones first seen cannot be shown the second time, even though all five cards (but the other side of each) were shown initially.

— Card Trick with a Tapered Deck —

Another simple trick to perform—but not easily detected—is executed by using a tapered deck of cards, as shown in *Figure 1.* A cheap deck of cards is evened up square, fastened in a vise, and planed along the edge in such a manner that the pack will be tapered about 1/16 in. This taper is exaggerated in the illustration, which shows one card that has been turned end to end.

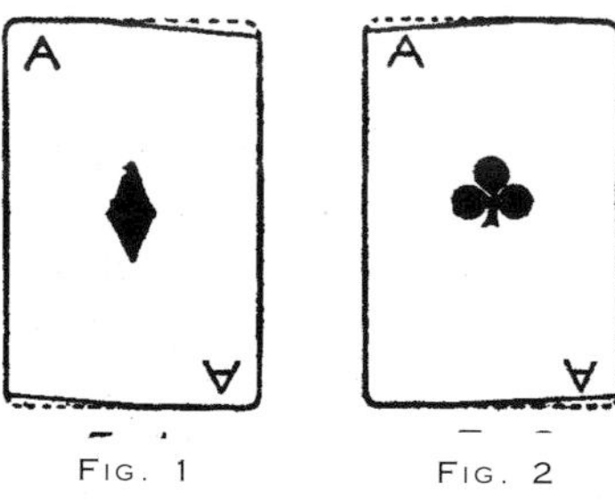

Fig. 1 Fig. 2

Cards from a tapered deck

It is evident that any card reversed in this way can be easily separated from the other cards in the pack, which makes it possible to perform the following trick: The performer spreads the cards out, like a fan, and asks an observer to withdraw a card. The card is then replaced in any part of the pack. After thoroughly shuffling the cards, the performer holds the deck in both hands behind his back and, pronouncing a few magic words, produces the selected card in one hand and the rest of the pack in the other.

This is accomplished by simply turning the deck end to end while the observer is looking at his card, thus putting the slightly wider end of the selected card at the narrow end of the pack when it is replaced. The hands are placed behind the back for a double purpose: the feat seems more marvelous, and the observers are not allowed to see how it is done.

In prize games, players having the same score are frequently called on to cut for low card to determine who wins. But a fairer way is to cut for high card, because a person familiar with the trick shown in *Figure 2* can cut the cards at the ace, deuce, or three spot nearly every time, especially if the deck is a new one. This is done by simply pressing on the top of the deck, as shown, before cutting the cards, thus causing the increased ink surface of the high cards to adhere to the adjacent ones. A little practice will soon enable a person to cut low nearly every time; however, the cards must be grasped lightly, and the experiment should be performed with a new deck to obtain successful results.

— A Magic Change Card —

Procure two cards, the 5 of diamonds and the 5 of spades, for example. Bend each exactly in the center, with the face of the cards on the inside, and then paste any card on the back, with its face against the two ends of the bent cards. The two opposite ends will then have their backs together, and these are also

A card having two faces, either of which can be shown to the audience instantly.

pasted. The illustration clearly shows this arrangement.

To perform the trick, pick up this card, which was placed in the pack beforehand, and show the audience both the front and back of the card. Be sure to keep the center part flat against one end or the other. Then pass a hand over the card, and in doing so catch the center part and turn it over. The card can be changed back again in the same manner.

— Card Levitation Impromptu —

This delightful novelty has puzzled many wise heads in the conjuring fraternity. The magician requests that two or three cards be chosen, which are returned to the pack and shuffled (with a pass and false shuffle). He then explains that, under certain conditions, it is possible to generate enough "magnetic influence" in the tip of his forefinger to "magnetize" a card. Suiting the action to the word, the conjurer rubs his forefingers together, then requests the name of the first chosen card, which, let us suppose, is the 2 of clubs.

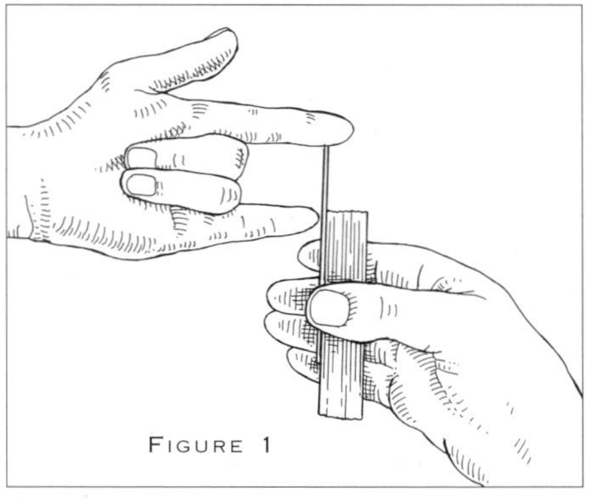

Figure 1

The pack is now held by its lower end, between the left thumb and fingers. The magician's right forefinger, held in the position of pointing, is placed about 1 in. above the pack. Slowly he raises it two or three times, without success. But the third time, the chosen card follows his finger out of the pack! This is repeated with the second card, and finally with the third. When the last card is halfway out of the pack, the conjurer removes his hand, and the card slowly sinks back into the pack. The magician explains that this is because the "magnetism" was broken, when his hand was removed. The cards are then passed around for examination.

Consulting the accompanying illustration (*Figure 1*) will make the solution clear: the extended little finger carries up the card. The illusion may be added to greatly by failing in the first two or three attempts. The latter part of the trick, that is, the descent of the card, is accomplished by a slight relaxation by the fingers and thumb of the left hand, which can easily be acquired after a few moments' practice.

— A Rising-Card Trick —

A rising-card trick can be accomplished with very little skill by using the simple device illustrated. The only things needed are four ordinary playing cards and a short rubber band. Pass one end of the rubber band through one card and the other end through the other card, as shown in the illustration, drawing the cards close together and fastening the ends by putting a pin through them. The remaining two cards are pasted to the first two so as to conceal the pins and ends of the rubber band.

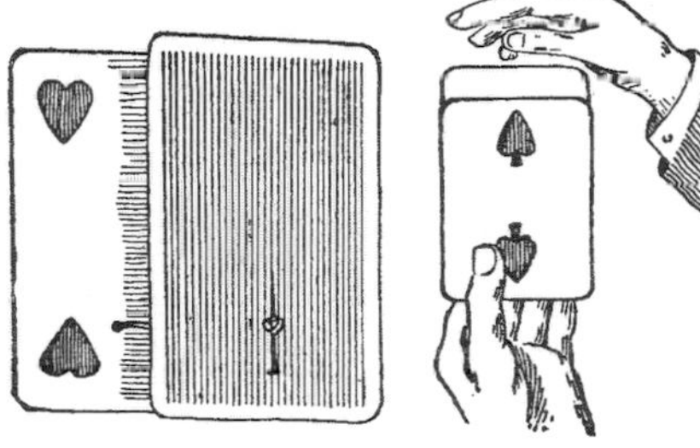

Card slips from the pack.

Put the cards with the rubber band in a pack of cards; take any other card from the pack and show it to the audience in such a way that you do not see and therefore know the card shown. Return the card to the pack—but be sure and place it between the cards tied together with the rubber band. Grasp the pack between your thumb and finger tightly at first; by gradually loosening your hold, you will make the card previously shown to the audience slowly rise out of the pack.

— Is This Your Card? —

A card is selected and then returned to the pack. The deck is cut a number of times. The performer deals the cards out in two

piles onto the extended hands of the spectator, requesting that the recipient say stop at any time. The signal is given. The performer asks for one of the piles and replaces it on the deck. The cards in the other pile are counted. "Nine?" The performer counts down to the ninth card in the deck. It is the selected card.

Do this: Take any playing card and gently crimp over the non-index corners, as shown in *Figure 1.* Place this card in the deck. Riffle the deck with your forefinger, as shown in *Figure 2.* Click! You automatically stop at the crimped card. That's the basic principle. *Figure 3* shows the start of the trick. The deck is on your hand, with the crimped card on the bottom. The spectator cuts the cards and looks at the top card of the pile in your hand, as shown in *Figure 4.* The selected card is then placed on the cut portion. The pile in your hand is placed onto the pile on the table. As a result, the crimped card is directly over the selected card.

The spectator cuts once and then again. This will bring the selected card roughly to the center of the pack. You cut the cards a third time. Use the riffle cut here, cutting at the "click." This brings the crimped card to the top of the pack, with the selected card immediately under it. Count the cards out, putting the first card on the spectator's left hand and continuing until the signal is given, ending with the right hand. Ask for one of the piles, as the same time extending your hand toward the right-hand heap—which, as you will remember, has the selected card on the bottom. The rest will just work itself out.

Cards *plus* Props

— Three-Pile Reveal —

Take twenty-one cards (any cards) from the pack and have these thoroughly shuffled. Deal them into three heaps, by adding one card at a time to each heap in turn. Continue this until all twenty-one have been dealt, making three packs of seven cards each. While this dealing is going on, a member of the audience has mentally chosen a card and noticed, at your request, into which heap of seven cards it has fallen. You now ask him to indicate to you the heap—not the card—in which his chosen card rests. Place this heap between the other two, with one above it and one below.

Deal a second time, asking him to select the same card mentally and, at the end of the second dealing, to indicate the heap in which it has now fallen. This heap is again placed between the other two, and the cards are dealt a third time. The same card is mentally chosen for the third time by your volunteer, and for a third time he indicates the heap in which it falls. Now, no matter what card he has chosen, if you have followed these instructions, the selected card will always be found to be the middle card of the heap as dealt for the third time. If, therefore, you have carefully noted the fourth or middle card of each heap when dealing for the third time, you will know immediately which card has been chosen. You may proceed to produce it when convenient, or to "read his mind" and tell him the card he has selected.

— The Ring-and-Card Trick —

The "Ring-and-Card Trick" is comparatively new and therefore more desirable.

A card is selected by the audience and given to the performer, who punches three holes in it, two on the top and one on the bottom (see illustration). Into those at the top, he strings a piece of cord or ribbon, then ties the ends to chairs placed about 4 ft. apart. Thus, the card is hanging with its face toward the audience. Into the third hole, the performer strings another short piece of ribbon, say, about 6 in. long. He ties the ends together, making a loop, which also hangs down.

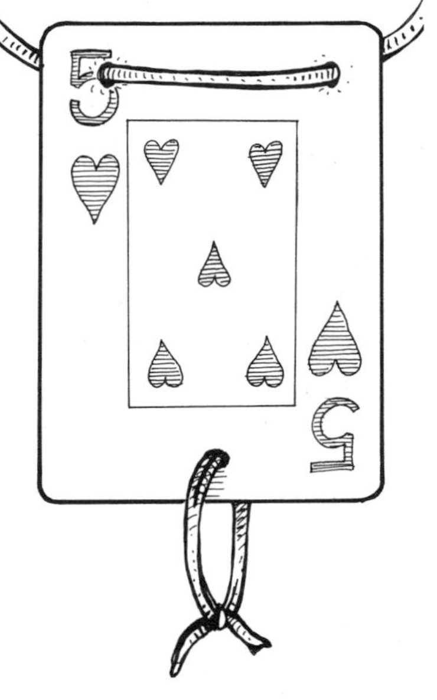

Next, a wedding ring is borrowed, and the performer, being duly impressed with his responsibility in having such a valuable article entrusted into his care, places it in a box and locks the box. Both are placed on a stand at some distance from the card. The performer then advances toward the box and, holding his wand at arm's length, taps the box gently with it. Whirling quickly, he also taps the card—and the ring is seen to appear, dangling in the free-hanging loop.

Now, it may seem an impossibility for a group of people, each presumably gifted with sound sight and excellent vision, to be so deceived. Nevertheless, the performer did not place the borrowed ring into the box, but palmed it instead. When the card was adjusted, and the upper string strung through it, a dummy wedding ring—one side of which had been well waxed or smeared with dry soap—was stuck to the back of the card directly over the lower hole. Thus, when the loop was threaded into the hole, it passed through the ring too. A very light tap with the wand was all that was needed to release it and cause it to fall down and become visible, dangling on the loop. In the act of untying the knot, the genuine ring is substituted for the dummy, to be returned and identified by its owner.

Another method of substitution is to thread the ring onto the wand, then offer it that way to the owner. The duplicate ring is threaded onto one end of the wand, while the real one is held palmed in the hand that is holding the wand. It can thereby, while still in the palm, be placed encircling the tip held in the hand. If the wand is transferred to the other hand, the real ring is presented, and the duplicate palmed.

A better method of having the ring appear is to have a black silk thread attached to it and held in the hand of an assistant behind the scenes. The magician in this case does not even approach the card to tap it, but simply makes a few passes with his hands, fires off a cap from a toy variety of pistol, or goes through some other ceremony. The ring, at the critical moment, appears.

— Card Caught on the End of a Walking Stick

A card is chosen by a member of the audience and then put back into the pack, and the whole pack is shuffled. All of the cards are then tossed into the air, the performer makes a slash at them with his walking stick, and behold! The card is seen to be dangling on the end of the walking stick when the shower of cards has subsided.

The stick itself is not prepared. But the performer has a loose ferrule, or metal cap, that just fits over the one on the stick, and which is removable at his pleasure. It will be seen, by referring to *Figure 1,* that on the lower end of this removable tip is a little loop, or staple, through which the performer may pass a black silk thread. The proper length of this

Figure 1

assistant tosses them all up in the air, as high as possible.

When the cards are thrown, the performer makes a slash with his stick. The thread is drawn taut, and the card is seen to be hanging on the point. The performer instantly grasps the loose intermediate position of the thread and brings it down into the right hand, which holds the cane; it is thus secured throughout its length against the stick. The left hand immediately travels to the tip and removes the card, and the string may be dropped where it will tell no tales.

thread will vary according to the height of the performer and the length of the stick used.

One end of the thread should be fastened to the upper button of the performer's vest, and the other end to the card that is to be caught. The card may rest in the pocket just inside the left side of the performer's coat, until it is wanted; the loose ferrule should be in the vest pocket.

A similar card is now forced on the audience by any of the usual methods, and when it is returned to the pack, the cards are shuffled. The performer, with stick in hand, takes his place with his right side to the audience. His assistant is opposite him, holding the cards. The walking stick is held at the "hanging guard position," the performer having previously taken an opportunity to slip the loose ferrule over the tip. He then asks the volunteer assistant to spread the pack like a fan, so that he may see the chosen card; when the performer says, "Three!" the

If the ferrule tapers fairly and has a small slit on each side, it will fit almost any stick. Thus, the effect of the trick may be heightened by using a borrowed stick. If an unsuitable stick is offered, it can be easily rejected as too long or too short, too heavy or too light, and another one borrowed in its stead. It is always wise, though, to have a stick of your own, so that you may use it if the proper kind cannot be secured from the audience.

This is a trick that demands careful practice beforehand. All the paraphernalia must be thoroughly tested and approved. If the thread is too

FIGURE 2

of stick, and the proper sweep to give in the slash should all be ascertained with exactitude before the amateur essays to perform it in public.

If desired, the performer may first of all "vanish" the desired card by placing it in the card box (*Figure 2*). This is a small box, the size of a playing card, painted black inside and provided with a loose "flap," also black (*a*).

long, the card will dangle some inches from the top of the stick; if the thread is too short and is broken by the slash, the card will fall to the ground with the others. Both cases will spoil the performance in a very lamentable manner. Therefore, the right length of thread, the right sort

With the card placed in the box, the lid (containing the flap) is closed, falling over the card and effectively concealing it. The box may now be shown, apparently empty. This little box may be employed in a number of different ways and is a useful piece of apparatus.

— Card Caught in the Handkerchief —

A card is selected—not forced—and then placed back in the deck, which is shuffled and held by a spectator. The performer now requests the loan of a gentleman's handkerchief, which he shows to be an ordinary one. The gentleman holding the pack is now requested to throw it in the air. As the cards descend, the performer waves the handkerchief among them, whereupon the chosen card is seen to be caught on its corner. Both are immediately passed around for inspection.

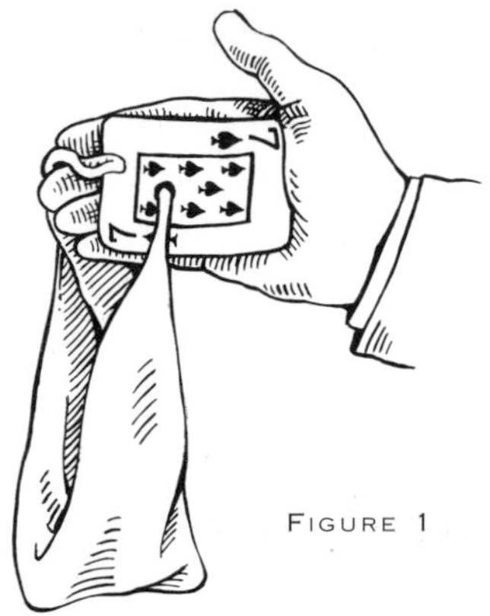

FIGURE 1

The following is the explanation of this effective little trick:

On the top vest button, the performer has a small portion of soft, adhesive wax. When the chosen card is returned, the performer places it on top of the pack, which is immediately handed back to the chooser to be shuffled. While placing the chosen card on the top of the pack, the performer quickly and secretly withdraws it, palming it in the hand. As the shuffling of the pack is going on, the performer removes the wax and sticks it to one corner of the palmed card.

A handkerchief is borrowed and held by two diagonal corners, with only the back of the hands being shown to the audience. The corner of the handkerchief is now pressed to the wax on the card (*Figure 1*). The cards are then thrown, and the performer, holding the two corners of the handkerchief between separate fingers, waves it among the falling cards. With a quick flap, he releases the palmed card. The handkerchief shoots out, the card becomes visible attached to its corner, and the effect is that the performer has actually caught one of the falling shower of cards (*Figure 2*).

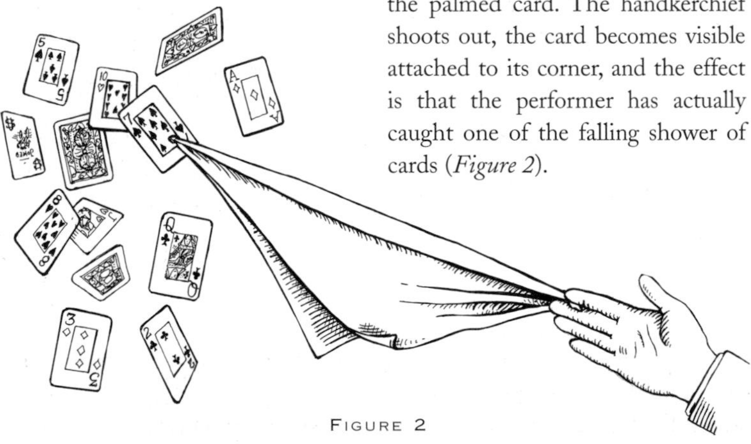

FIGURE 2

— The Enchanted Card Frame —

A mystifying card trick in which the performer makes use of the enchanted card frame shown in detail in the illustration, this is performed as follows: A pack of playing cards is given to one of the spectators, who selects a card, noting the number and suit. The card is then placed in an envelope and burned by the spectator. The performer takes the ashes and loads them into a cap pistol, which he aims at a small frame that is shown to be empty and is set on a table a few feet distant. The frame is covered with a handkerchief, and the pistol is fired at it. When the performer removes the handkerchief, the selected and destroyed card appears in the frame, from which it is taken at the back.

The trick is performed as follows: A forced deck is prepared having twenty-four like cards, and the backs of the cards are held toward the spectators when a card is selected. The frame is made of molding 2 in. wide, mitered at the corners, and of the size indicated. The opening of the frame is 6⅜ by 7½ in. The general views of the frame in normal position and inverted are shown in *Figures 1* and *5*. A pocket is cut in the lower edge of the frame at the back,

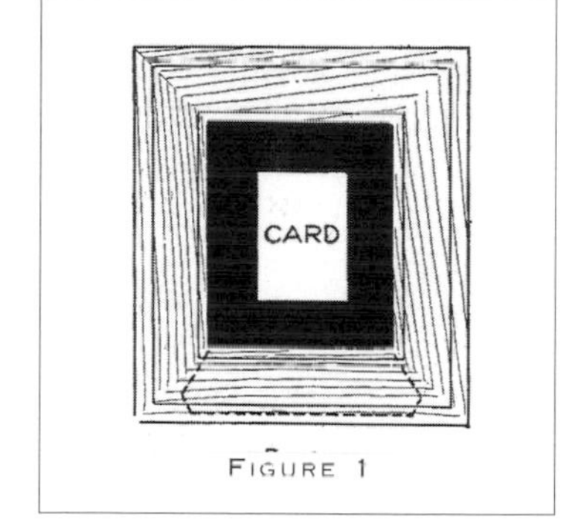

Figure 1

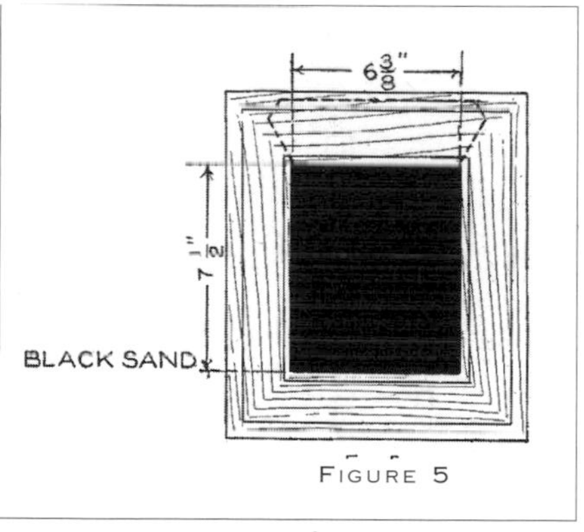

Figure 5

A pocket is cut into the frame and filled with black sand, obscuring the card when the frame is inverted.

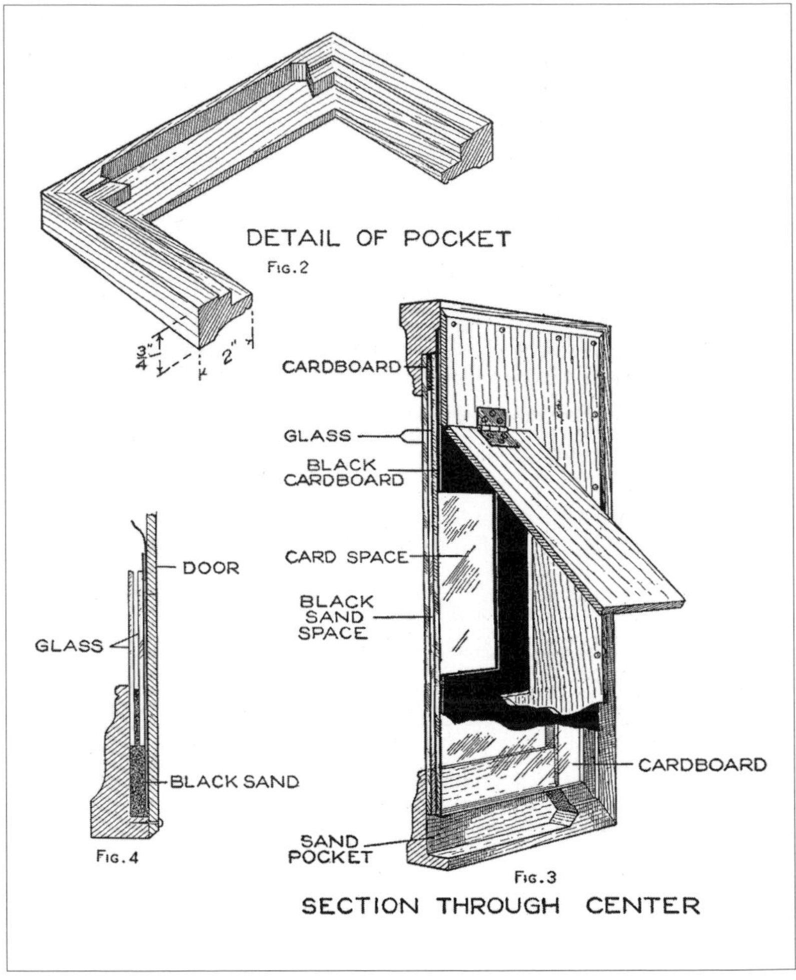

as shown in detail in *Figure 2.* A pane of glass is fitted into the frame, and on the three edges other than the one having a pocket, ⅛ in.-thick strips of cardboard are glued as a bearing for the second piece of glass, as shown in *Figure 4*. The back of the frame is fitted with a cover of thin wood, and a hinged door is arranged in the center of the back, as shown in *Figure 3*.

A mat of black cardboard is fitted into the frame to form a background behind the card (*Figure 1*). The pocket at the bottom is filled with black sand—a kind used by sign painters is satisfactory—and the frame is ready to receive the card for the performance of the trick. One of the cards from the forced deck is placed in the frame. By inverting the latter, the sand is caused to run between the glass partitions, concealing the card on the black mat behind it. In this condition, it is exhibited to the spectators and then placed on the table. A handkerchief is thrown over it, and the cap pistol is fired at it. In picking up the frame, the performer turns it over while removing the handkerchief, so that the black sand runs back into the pocket in the frame.

{CHAPTER 2}

TOOLS *of the* TRADE

USEFUL DEVICES

— THE MAGIC CAVE —

You are seated in a parlor at night with the lights turned low. In front of you, between the parlor and the room in back of it, is an upright square of brightly burning lights surrounding a perfectly black space. The magician stands in front of this, in his shirtsleeves, and after a few words of introduction proceeds to show the wonders of his magic cave. Showing you plainly that both hands are empty, he points with one finger to the box, where immediately there appears a small white china bowl. He holds his empty hand over this bowl, and some oranges and apples drop from that hand into the bowl. He removes the bowl from the black box, or cave, and hands its contents round to the audience. Receiving the bowl again, he tosses it into the cave, but it never reaches the floor—it disappears in midair.

The illusions he shows you are too many to detail at length. Objects appear and disappear. Heavy metal objects, such as forks, spoons, and

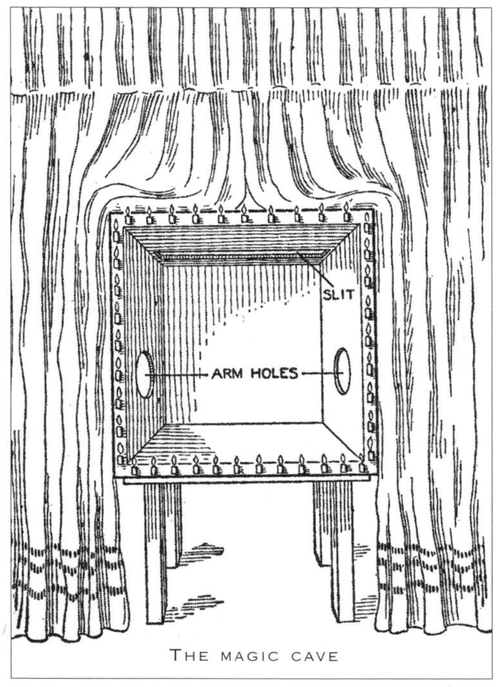

THE MAGIC CAVE

jackknives, which have been shown to the audience and can have no strings attached to them, fly about in the box at the will of the operator. One thing changes to another and back again, and black art reigns supreme.

Now, all of this "magic" is very simple and requires no more skill to prepare or execute than any clever boy or girl of fourteen may possess. It is based on the performance of the famous Herrmann, and it relies on a principle of optics for its success. To prepare such a magic cave, the requisites are a large soapbox, a few simple tools, some black paint, some black cloth, and plenty of candles.

The box must first be altered. One end is removed, and a slit, ⅓ of the length from the remaining end, is cut in one side. This slit should be as long as the width of the box and about 5 in. wide. On either side of the box, halfway from open end to closed end, should be cut a hole, just large enough to comfortably admit a hand and arm.

Next, the box should be painted black, both inside and out, and then lined inside with black cloth. This lining must be done neatly—no folds must show, and no heads of tacks. The interior must be a dead black. The box is painted black first, so the cloth used need not be very heavy; but if the cloth is sufficiently thick, no painting inside is required. The whole inside is to be cloth-lined: floor, top, sides, and end.

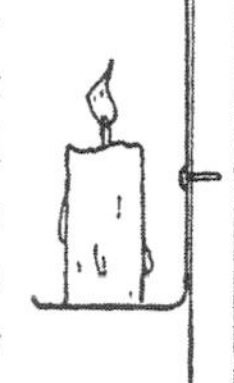

After that, the illumination in front must be arranged. A plentiful supply of short candles will do. The candles must be close together and arranged on little brackets around the whole front of the "cave," and they should have little pieces of bright tin behind them, to throw the light toward the audience. The whole function of these candles is to dazzle the eyes of the spectators, heighten the illusion, and prevent them from seeing very far into the black box.

Finally, you must have an assistant, who must be provided with either black gloves or black bags to go over his hands and arms. And you need several black drop curtains, attached to sticks greater in length than the width of the box. These are let down through the slit in the top.

The audience room should have only low lights; the room where the cave is should be dark, and if you can drape portieres (curtains hung across doorways) between two rooms around the box (which, of course, is on a table), so much the better.

The whole secret of the trick lies in the fact that if light is turned away from anything black, into the eyes of someone who is looking at it, the much fainter light reflected from the black surface will not affect the observer's eye. Consequently, when the exhibitor puts his hand in the cave, and his confederate behind inserts his own hand covered with a black glove and holding a small bag of black cloth, in which there are oranges and apples, then pours them from the bag into a dish, the audience sees the oranges and apples appear but does not see the black arm and bag against the black background.

The dish appears by having been placed in position behind a black curtain, which is snatched swiftly away at the proper moment by the assistant. Any article thrown into the cave and caught by the black hand and concealed by a black cloth seems to disappear. Any object not too large can be made to "levitate" by the same means. A picture of anyone present may be made to change into a grinning skeleton by suddenly screening it with a dropped curtain, while another curtain is swiftly removed from over a pasteboard skeleton, which can be made to dance either by strings or by the black veiled hand holding on to it from behind. The skeleton can then change to, say, a white cat.

But illusions suggest themselves. There is no end to the effects that can be had from this simple apparatus, and if the operators are sufficiently well drilled, the result is truly remarkable to the uninitiated. The illusion, as presented by Herrmann, was identical to this one. Only he, of course, had a big stage, and people clothed in black to creep about and do his bidding. Here, the power behind the throne is but a black-veiled hand and arm. It can be made even more complicated by having two assistants, one on each side of the box; this is the reason why it was advised that two holes be cut. This enables an absolutely instantaneous change, as one uncovers one object at the moment the second assistant covers and removes the other.

It is important that the assistants remain invisible throughout; if portieres are impossible, a screen must be used to block nearby light. But any boy ingenious enough to follow these simple instructions will not need to be told that the whole success of the exhibition depends on the absolute failure of the audience to understand that there is more than one person concerned with bringing about the curious effects that are seen. The exhibitor should be a boy who can talk; a good "patter"—as the magicians call it—is often of more value than a whole host of mechanical effects and helpers. It is essential that the exhibitor and his confederate be well drilled, so that the latter can produce the proper effects at the proper cue from the former. Finally, never give an exhibition with the "cave" until you have watched the illusions from the front yourself. This way you can determine whether everything connected with the draping is right, or whether some stray bit of light reveals what you wish to conceal.

— The Mirrored Tumbler —

One of the most useful magic devices in the magician's bag is the glass tumbler, partitioned by a mirror through the center.

This piece of apparatus, in its simplest form, is just an ordinary tumbler. It is preferably one having a stand, and sides fluted at the top, with a small mirror of movable patent glass. The silvered side is protected by a coat of varnish, and thus it may contain any liquid without injury to the mirror. When the glass is placed with the mirror facing squarely toward the audience, there is no reason to suppose that the glass is not thoroughly transparent, while in reality the other compartment may contain anything from a bouquet of flowers to a silk handkerchief.

Thus, if the performer wishes to produce, say, a glass of sweets from an empty tumbler, he merely fills the invisible compartment with the candies and places the mirror in the center; to the audience, the glass will appear to be perfectly empty. The handkerchief may then be placed over it for an instant, with the mirror grasped by the thumb and index finger and revolved with the handkerchief. The candies are thus revealed—and they may be quickly distributed.

The mirror may also be made double, which allows both sides of the tumbler to be shown at different intervals, without suspicion being aroused. Thus, if it is desired to change a guinea pig into a rabbit, a large glass bowl is provided. One animal is placed in one of the compartments, the second animal in the other. All that is necessary to effect this change is a twist of the glass, which brings the other half toward the spectators with the other animal visible. Provided that both of the animals are sufficiently docile, the trick is achieved. If it is desired to exchange two handkerchiefs, this double mirror again becomes effective, and only a twist of the glass is necessary. Indeed, if the performer is perfectly at ease, he may not need to cover the tumbler at all but, simply taking it up from the table, may transfer it from one hand to the other, thus bringing about the necessary twist by means of a semicircle described by the arm.

THE TUMBLER WITH TWO COMPARTMENTS

It is wise, in the case of the double mirror, to have it lined with felt. This should project about ⅛ in. beyond the silvered glass. This prevents any rattling, and it also causes the mirror to fit with greater snugness.

The secret compartment is also a very useful place in which to deposit small articles that, having served their turn, are no longer required. With an apparently careless movement, the article may be dropped into the hindmost compartment, and the glass is removed shortly after by an assistant, who then makes the necessary disposition of the article for the purposes of the trick being presented.

— The Bottomless Tumbler —

The next manufactured property that the conjurer will find to be a friend in need is what is known as the "bottomless tumbler." This is purely and simply an ordinary tumbler, the bottom of which has been removed. The use of such a piece of apparatus is obvious. For instance, a borrowed article such as a glove is plainly dropped into the glass, which the performer holds at arm's length in his hand. A cover is now placed over the glass for an instant, and the whole deposited upon a stand. The glove, which appears to be so safe within the tumbler, may, of course, be easily palmed by the conjurer. It is thus caused to appear at any convenient moment in some entirely unsuspected place, while the performer has not approached the glass since placing it on a stand in full view of the spectator. An egg, a ball, a watch, or a folded handkerchief—in fact, any article—may be treated in just the same manner.

An improvement on this is the following: Instead of removing the whole bottom, remove a circular disk from it, thus leaving a rim of about ½ in. all around. This rim will keep many articles within the glass while it is being shown, and the hand of the conjurer does not need to be kept continually under the bottom.

This will even allow the performer to pour water into the glass to show that it is entirely without preparation. To do this, the bottom of the glass will have to be absolutely flat, and a thin disk fitting both into and over the bottom must be provided. If a little grease, such as Vaseline, is spread over the lower edges, the glass will be quite watertight, so long as the disk is kept from shifting. If the finger is held under the glass, this contingency will be provided for. After the water is poured out, or drunk, the glass may be wiped and the disk and Vaseline removed at the same time.

— The Vanisher —

The very useful "vanisher" is also a good device for the would-be magician to provide for himself. This appliance is made of tin, circular in shape, about ¾ in. in diameter, and the same in depth. One segment of this hollow circular disk of metal is cut off, together with the accompanying part of its side, and an opening formed (see illustration). A small, sharp hook projects from one side. After the handkerchief is worked into the receptacle, the whole may be hung on the back of a chair or hooked into a table cover or any drapery that happens to be handy or to the performer's clothes, as may be desirable. If one of its flat sides is smeared with glue, this box may even be stuck to the back of the performer's hand.

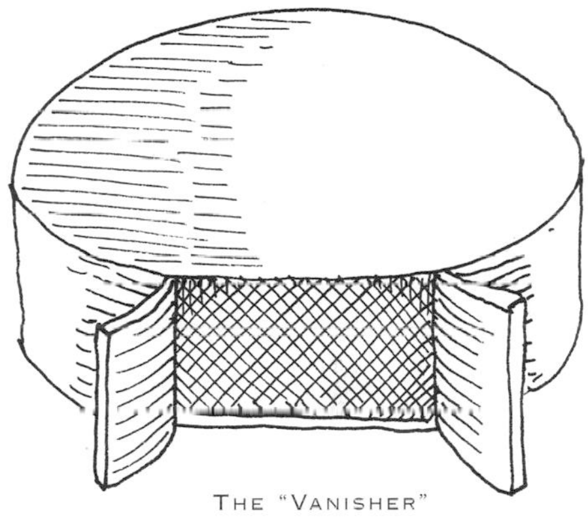

The "Vanisher"

The amateur conjurer can make one of these little boxes for himself with strips of cardboard. The two side pieces are first cut out to the required shape. Then a strip, about ½ in. wide, is bent round and fastened solidly between the two side pieces by means of adhesive tape. The whole is now painted flesh color, and a piece of magician's wax is stuck on one side of the box. If the handkerchief is now worked into this box, the latter may be moved over on the ends of the second and third fingers of the right hand, under cover of the left, and stuck onto the back of the left hand. The handkerchief and box are now out of sight. The hand may be held open, as before, while the fingers of the right hand "work," as though containing the handkerchief, and are finally shown empty. Or a fine loop of thin catgut may be attached to the upper ends of the box; this, slung over the thumb of the left hand, will effectively hold the box in place.

— The Bran Glass —

A glass of bran may be instantly changed to a glass of sweets, or any other article, in this manner:

The performer brings forward a glass of bran, and to prove that it is such, he scatters some on the floor. A cover, which has been examined by the audience, is then placed over the goblet. Upon its removal, the bran is nowhere to be seen. Instead, the glass is full of candies, nuts, and the like, which are scattered among the audience and readily demolished by the youngsters present, in spite of the mystery surrounding their presence and their magic appearance.

Turning Bran into Candy

A hollow cardboard shape is made to fit inside the glass, which is generally a goblet, large or small, according to whether it's intended for stage or drawing-room use. The cardboard shape is open only at the bottom, and outside bran is glued on so that, when placed in a goblet, it appears to be a glass full of bran. The hollow inside of the cardboard shape is first filled with sweets or, if preferred, some borrowed article, then placed in the glass (see illustration). A cover, generally made of brass, with the sides tapering outward, is made to go over the goblet. When pressed down hard, the rim of the bran-covered shape becomes jammed; then, when the cover is raised, the bran shape also rises, unseen, and the sweets or other articles are left in the glass. Some loose bran is always heaped on the top of the tin shape, and blown to the floor at the commencement, so as to disarm suspicion. If preferred, a borrowed handkerchief may be employed, instead of the cover. In this case, the top rim of the bran-covered shape is palmed through the handkerchief and removed with it.

— The Drawer Box —

This is a piece of apparatus that is frequently used in magic and looks very much like the individual files used for card indexes. It consists of a drawer (*a*) with a small knob on the outside, used to remove it. This drawer contains (*b*) a coverless wooden box, only a trifle smaller than the drawer, and fitting into it with perfect snugness. The drawer itself has no back, only three sides and a base. Thus, it may be withdrawn together with the telescoped box, or without it, as the needs of the moment require. If it is desired to show the drawer empty, it is pulled out to its entire length so that nothing can be seen—while the box, which remains inside the case, may contain anything from a pack of cards to a live rabbit (see illustration).

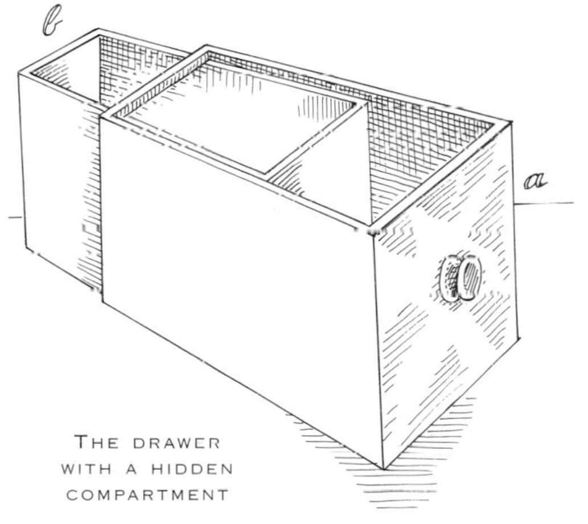

The drawer with a hidden compartment

The manner of controlling the movements of the box is very ingenious. The base of the case, which is covered with thick felt, contains a delicate spring connected with a catch, or stud, to the inside of the drawer. The stud corresponds with a small groove on the base of the box. When the catch is pressed by the performer from the outside, the stud falls into the groove, fastening the box to the drawer. In this way, the box is withdrawn with its contents when the drawer is removed. The inner box is made of such thin pieces of wood that a casual observer would not notice the difference in the thickness of the drawer, with or without it. Besides, the upper edges of the drawer are slightly turned over at the top, which further conceals the presence of the inner compartment when they are withdrawn together.

— The Inexhaustible Portfolio —

This is an ordinary-looking portfolio, similar to those used to accommodate music or drawings. It is shown to be perfectly empty, but when placed on the table, with its back to the audience, the performer is able to produce from it a variety of the most diverse objects. From time to time, it is again shown to be empty, then once more the productive process is repeated (*Figure 1*).

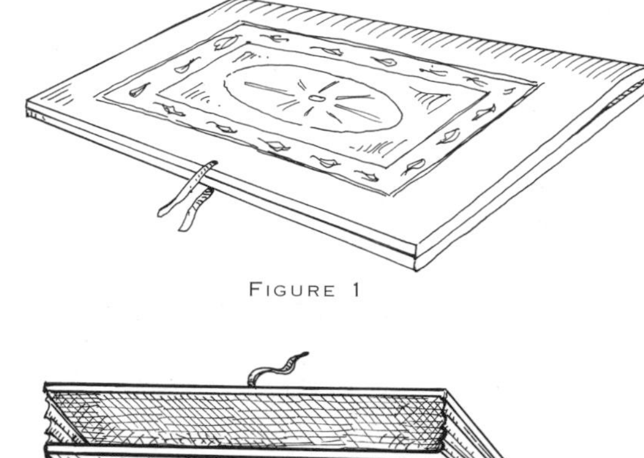

Figure 1

Figure 2

The external decoration of the portfolio takes the shape of a panel on one side of it. This panel forms a trap, closed by an inner cover, or intermediate leaf, to which the panel is glued. When the portfolio is first opened to show it empty, the accordion sides of the trap lie flat against the lower side, and the trap is closed. But when the portfolio is laid open on the table for the performance of the trick, it is opened with the intermediate leaf against the upper side, leaving the trap open (*Figure 2*). The portfolio is drawn partly off the table, and the opening is thereby brought over the *servante* (a shelf attached to the back of the main performing table and concealed by it), enabling the performer to thrust his hand through and bring up the objects to be produced, which beforehand have been placed on the hidden shelf.

— A HOMEMADE MAGIC LANTERN —

The essential parts of a magic lantern are a condensing lens to make the beam of light converge on the slide to illuminate it evenly, a projecting lens with which to throw an enlarged picture of the illuminated slide on a screen, and some appliances for preserving the proper relation of these parts to each other. The best of materials should be used and the parts put together with care to produce a clear picture on the screen.

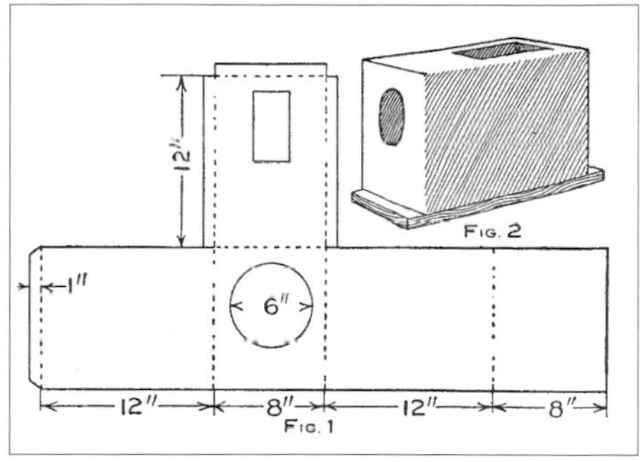

LANTERN HOUSE

The first part to make is the lamp house, or box, to hold the light. The illustration shows the construction for an electric light, but the same box may be used for gas or an oil lamp, provided the material is metal. A tin box with dimensions close to those given in the diagram may be secured from your local grocer. But if such a box is not found, one can be made from a piece of tin, cut as shown in *Figure 1.* When this metal is bent at right angles on the dotted lines, it will form a box as shown in *Figure 2,* which is placed on a baseboard, ½ to ¾ in. thick, 8 in. wide, and 14 in. long. This box should be provided with a reflector located just in back of the lamp.

Procure a plano-convex or biconvex 6 in. lens with a focal length of from 15 to 20 in., as well as a projecting lens 2 in. in diameter with a focal length such that it will provide a picture of the required size. Or you can use a lens of 12 in. focus, enlarging a 3 in. slide to about 6 ft. at a distance of 24 ft.

The woodwork of the lantern should be ½ in., well-seasoned pine, white wood, or walnut, and the parts should be fastened together with wood screws, wire brads, or glue, as desired. The board on which the condensing lens is mounted should be 16 in. wide and 15 in. high, battened on both ends to keep the wood

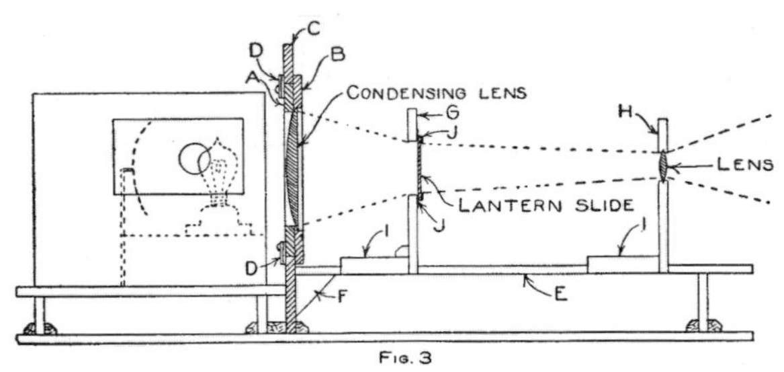

FIG. 3

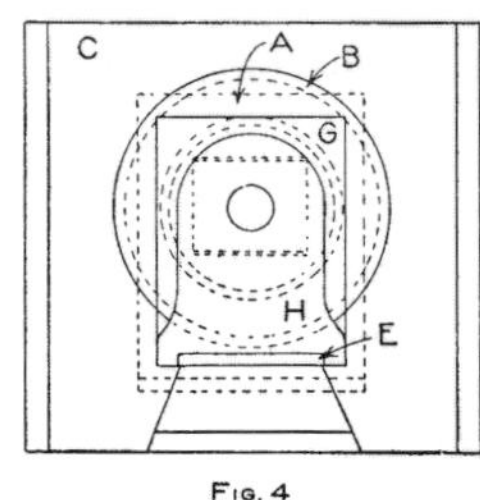

FIG. 4

MAGIC LANTERN DETAILS

from warping. The board is centered both ways. At a point 1 in. above the center, describe a 9 in. circle with a compass and saw the wood out with a scroll or keyhole saw. If a small saw is used and the work carefully done, the circular piece removed will serve to make the smaller portion of the ring that holds the condensing lens. This ring is actually made up from two rings, *A* and *B* in *Figures 3* and *4*. The inside and outside diameters of ring *B* are ⅜ in. greater than the corresponding diameters of ring *A*, so that when they are fastened together concentrically, an inner rabbet (or groove) is formed for the reception of the lens and an outer rabbet to fit against the board, *C*. This is the board in and against which it rotates, being held in place by buttons, *DD*.

A table, *E*, about 2 ft. long, is fastened to the board, *C*, with brackets, *F*, and supported at the outer end with a standard. The slide support, *G*, and the lens slide, *H*, are constructed to slip easily on the table, *E*, with the strips, *II*, serving as guides. Small strips of tin, *JJ*, are bent as shown and fastened at the top and bottom of the rectangular opening cut in the support, *G*, for holding the lantern slides.

All the parts should be joined together snugly and the movable parts made to slide freely. When all is complete and well sandpapered, apply two coats of shellac varnish and place the lamp house on the bottom board behind the condensing lens; the lantern is then ready for use.

The proper light and focus may be obtained by slipping the movable parts on board *C*. When the right position is found for each, all slides will produce a clear picture on the screen, if the positions of the lantern and the screen are not changed.

Fun *with* Black Thread

— The Magnetized Poker —

It has often been said that a black silk thread is "the conjurer's best friend." A great number of tricks can be performed with its aid. One of the most amusing, and at the same time one of the simplest, feats is known as the "Magnetized Poker." A black thread is attached to the trouser legs at the knees, the length being suited to the legs of the performer, and varying from 6 to 12 in. long. When the knees are separated, this thread becomes taut. If a poker is leaned against the thread, it will remain in an upright position, kept so by the thread. The performer should make as many passes over the poker as necessary to "magnetize" it before the trick commences, and effective patter is essential for the successful production of this simple feat.

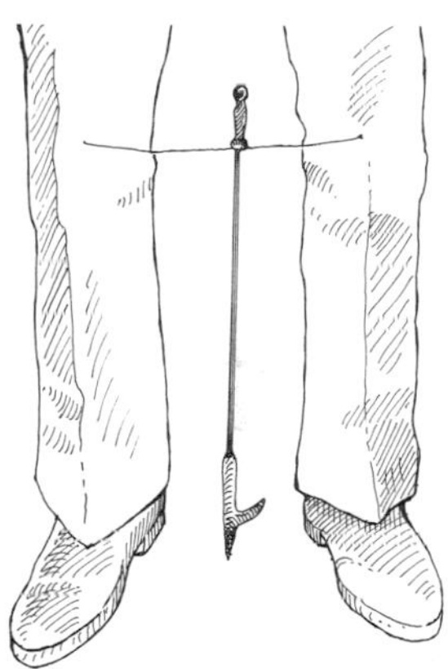

The poker leans against the thread.

— The Dancing Handkerchief —

Another illusion, known as "The Dancing Handkerchief," is also accomplished by means of a thread. The simplest way of performing this is merely to have a black silk thread attached to a handkerchief and running over a pulley in the ceiling. The fundamental objection to this, however, is that nearly everyone at once suspects that a thread is being employed. To offset this and to enable the performer to pass his hands above and below the handkerchief while it is dancing about, he resorts to the following device: A black thread is stretched entirely across the stage; one end of this is attached to a hook about 18 in. from the ground, with the other end in the hand of an assistant. When not in use, this thread is allowed to lie slack, and it will remain on the carpet invisible. The instant it is pulled taut, however, it rises to a height of some 18 in. or more. The handkerchief, which was carelessly thrown over this thread, naturally rises with it, and it dances about in its well-known amusing manner.

— The Rapping Wand —

This principle also explains the tricks known as the "Rapping Wand" and the "Rapping Hand." In both these cases, a black silk thread is stretched entirely across the stage and is elevated by the assistant, who stands well hidden behind a screen. In the first case, the wand is merely placed over the thread, and it naturally rises an inch or two whenever the thread is slightly tightened. It comes down onto the table with an audible thud, which is interpreted as a "rap."

— The Mesmerized Wand —

The performer shows his hand to be empty and passes his wand around for inspection. When it is returned to him, it will apparently remain attached to his fingertips in any position he may desire.

For this trick, it is necessary to have a silk thread previously tied at one end to the top button of your waistcoat and at the other end to the bottom button. After the wand is returned to the performer, the hand

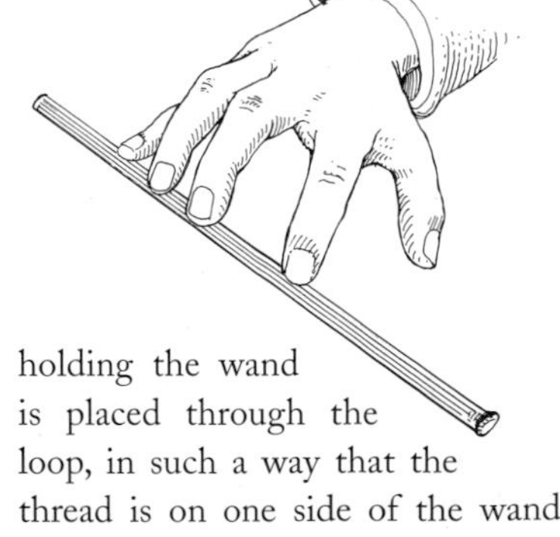

holding the wand is placed through the loop, in such a way that the thread is on one side of the wand

and the pressure of the fingers on the other. Thus, by pressing your hand against it, the wand will seemingly lie horizontally in the air, as though stuck to the palm of the hand. The stick may be shifted to almost any position, and if the pressure of the fingers is sufficient, it will remain without any visible support.

— The Climbing Ring —

The black thread is also responsible for the raising and lowering of a borrowed ring, placed over the magician's wand. The wand has a needle slightly projecting from one end, and over this is slipped a loop of black thread. The other end of the thread is attached to the top button of the performer's waistcoat. A borrowed ring having been slipped over the wand, it naturally carries with it a certain "slack" of the black silk thread. All the performer has to do, therefore, in order to cause the ring to rise upward is to push the wand (held in an upright position) farther from his body or, with the other hand, depress the slack that exists between his body and the wand. This will cause the ring to rise until it reaches the top of the wand, where it may be removed and at once handed around for inspection.

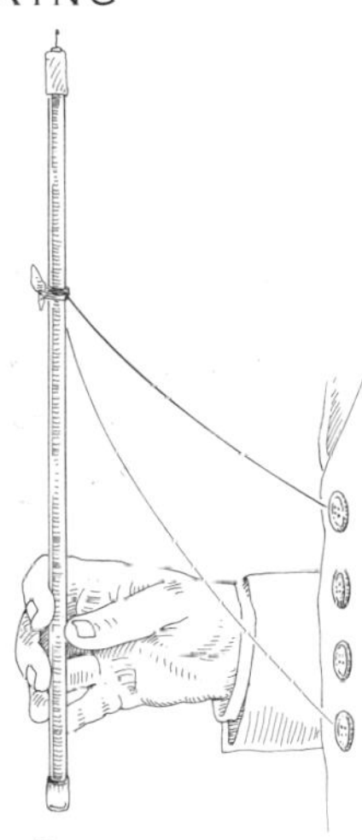

Raising the Ring

— The Lifting Table —

The "Lifting Table" may be introduced as a mesmeric effect. A small, three-legged or other lightweight table is used, preferably covered with plush or velvet. A fringe hangs around it. A pin has been driven in the center of the table, with the head and about ⅛ in. of the stem projecting. This will be invisible in the midst of the plush. A finger ring, worn on the second or third finger of the right hand, has a little groove cut into it, all the way through to the finger. The head of the pin may thus be slipped inside, so that the stem projects through the groove, and the table will then be maintained by steadying it with the other fingers of the hand.

The table is shown to the audience, and the hands are exhibited and wiped to prove that they are empty and without glue. After the usual passes, the hands are lowered to the table, the pin is slid into the groove in the ring, and the table is lifted. After swinging it around in various ways, one hand is removed. Finally, advance to the audience, give the table a twist, turning it upside down, and with a quick jerk (apparently to show that there is nothing underneath), remove the pin from the table, by means of the ring, before handing over the table for immediate examination. While this is going on, remove the pin from your ring by the thumb of the same hand and show that your hands are empty.

An additional effect may be produced by suddenly affecting to hear that glue or electricity was used to perform the feat. To prove that neither was employed, take out a large silk handkerchief and smooth it over the top—at the same time, of course, causing the pin to penetrate it. Then slide the pin in the groove and elevate the table as before, removing the pin at the end of the demonstration and offering the handkerchief and table for examination.

An ordinary wooden chair may be lifted by this means—or even a large wooden table by using two rings, with a needle driven into either end.

— The Floating Hat —

The "Floating Hat" is another illusion produced with the aid of the black thread. A loop some 2 ft. long is passed over the magician's head and neck, hanging in front of him but invisible against his black clothes. A hat, having been

borrowed, is dexterously passed through the loop, mouth downward, and the performer, by placing his fingers upon the crown of the hat and pressing downward, is able to raise it and apparently cause it to remain suspended in space, without visible means of support.

Sleight *of* Handkerchief

— Handkerchief Mended after Being Cut and Torn —

Two people are requested to come forward from the audience to hold the four corners of a handkerchief. Then beg several other handkerchiefs from the audience and place them on the one held by the two individuals. When several handkerchiefs have been accumulated, have someone draw one out from the bunch and examine it for any marks, which will determine that this handkerchief is the one to be mended after being mutilated. This person, as well as others, will then cut off pieces from this marked handkerchief and finally tear it apart.

The pieces are all collected, and some magic spirits are thrown over the torn and cut parts. Tie them in a small package with a ribbon and put them under a glass, which you warm up with your hands. After a few seconds' time, you remove the glass, which you have held all the time, and take out the handkerchief and unfold it—whereupon everyone will recognize the previously noticed mark on it and be amazed not to find a cut or tear in the texture.

This trick is very simple: You have an understanding in advance with someone in the group, who has two handkerchiefs that are exactly alike and has given one of them to a person behind the curtain. He throws the other, at the time of the request for handkerchiefs, onto the handkerchiefs held for use in the performance of the trick. You manage to keep this handkerchief where it will be picked out in preference over the others, though pretending to mix them up thoroughly. The person selected to pick out a handkerchief naturally will take the handiest one. Be sure that this is the right one.

When the handkerchief has been torn and folded, put it under the glass, on a table, near a partition or curtain. The table should be made with a hole cut through the top and a small trapdoor fitted snugly in the hole, so that it will appear to be a part of the tabletop. This trapdoor is hinged on the underside and opens into the drawer of the table; it can be operated by the person behind the curtain, who will remove the torn handkerchief and replace it with the good one, then close the trapdoor by reaching through the drawer of the table.

— Handkerchief from Thin Air —

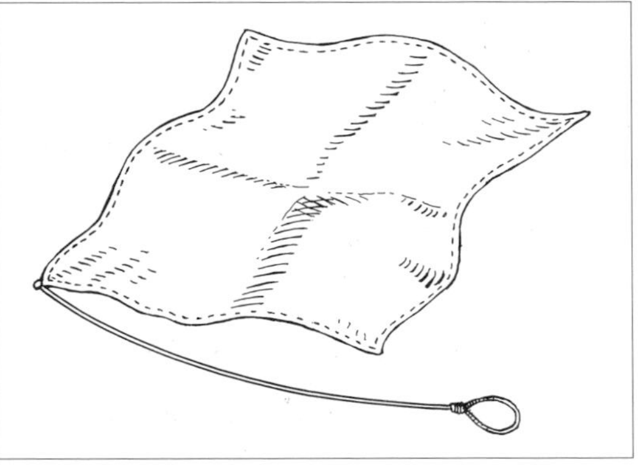

In the next trick to be explained, the performer rolls up his sleeves, shows that his hands are empty, both back and front, then waves his hands in the air and produces a large silk handkerchief or flag.

This is effected as follows: Procure a watch swivel and a piece of the very finest wire. Make a loop of the wire about 2½ in. long and fasten it to the ring of the watch swivel. Fold up the handkerchief, as small as possible, and fasten the watch swivel where the folds come together. Place the handkerchief under your waistcoat and allow the wire loop to project outside. If the wire is fine enough, it will be unnoticeable. In waving your hand from one side to the other, catch your left thumb in the loop so that, by a slight pull, the handkerchief falls into your palm. Bring both hands together and produce the handkerchief. Immediately pass it around for examination, at the same time making away with the hook. Immediately afterward, show your hands to be perfectly empty.

— The Candle and the Handkerchief —

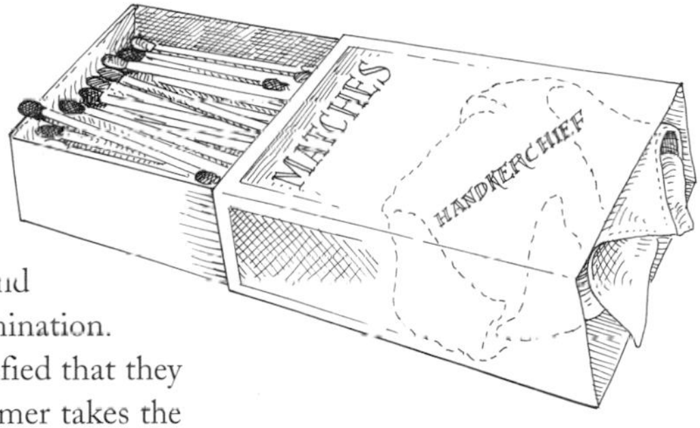

The following is one of the showier tricks and therefore a good program piece. A silk handkerchief and a candle are passed around the audience for examination. When everyone is satisfied that they are genuine, the performer takes the handkerchief and rolls it into a ball—whereupon it vanishes from his hands, which are shown to be empty. He then goes to the candle and produces a handkerchief from its flame.

To perform this feat, procure two small silk handkerchiefs, exactly alike. Folding one up neatly, tie it around with a piece of weak cotton. Take an ordinary box of matches (which can be slid open at either end), half-open it, and place the folded handkerchief in the space left by the box proper after sliding out the inner container holding the matches (see illustration). The box is then placed on the table, with the handkerchief side away from the audience. Any ordinary candle may be used.

The second handkerchief is handed out with the candle for examination, and when returned it is rolled up and vanished by palming it. It is palmed in the right hand, but the left is kept closed to lead the audience into thinking that it holds the handkerchief. Holding this closed left hand in the air, lean over, and reach for your wand with your right hand. In doing so, drop the palmed handkerchief on your servante. Then pretend to throw the contents of the left hand toward the candle; open the left hand in doing so, now showing both hands to be empty.

Now go to the candle and announce that you will light it. For this purpose, take a match from the box, strike it, and close the box—thus forcing the concealed handkerchief out the open other end of the box into your palm, where it is retained.

Lift out the candle with the same hand and approach the audience, making various catches at the flame with the left hand, grabbing at it quickly and darting back. Suddenly, pretend to draw out the handkerchief, closing the left hand and dropping the candle quickly, then bring your hands together to reveal the handkerchief.

— The Soup Plate and the Handkerchief —

For the next trick, the performer needs two handkerchiefs, which he shows together with an empty soup plate. He places the plate upside down on the table after spreading a newspaper beneath it—saying that it's "in order to prevent any idea of assistance from below." He then takes the two handkerchiefs between his hands. They disappear, after which, on lifting the soup plate with the tips of his fingers, the performer discloses both handkerchiefs beneath it.

The neatest way of vanishing the handkerchief is the method of using a small, concealed black bag as described previously. If this is not large enough to hold them both, vanish one by another means already described. To cause them to appear under the soup plate, cut out a round piece of cardboard to fit the bottom of the plate exactly. On one side of the cardboard, paste newspaper, and on the other side, highly glazed white paper. From a short distance, this will look like the china itself. Place two duplicate handkerchiefs in the bottom of the plate and cover them over with the false bottom, glazed side up. When this is held toward the audience, it will appear to be the bottom of the plate itself.

The false bottom should be a little loose, sufficiently so to enable it to fall out when the plate is inverted. It can be kept in place by the fingers while exhibiting the plate to the spectators. It will be remembered that the underside of the false bottom is covered with newspaper. Therefore, when the plate is inverted and the false bottom falls out, there being a newspaper underneath the plate, the audience will still be unaware of any trickery. The handkerchiefs will be discovered to be lying under the plate, which may be handed around for examination.

— The Shower of Sweets —

The following is a very antiquated trick, but one that is always hailed with acclaim from the juvenile portion of the audience. The performer borrows a handkerchief and spreads it on his table. He then lifts it by nipping it between his forefinger and thumb. A lady is asked to breathe on it, and a perfect shower of small candies and sweetmeats falls on a plate held underneath to catch them.

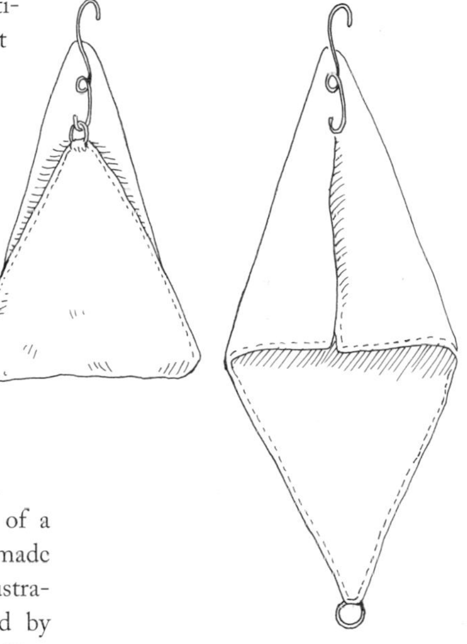

Unhook the flap to release the shower of sweets.

The secret lies in the use of a small bag of muslin or calico, made of the shape shown in the illustration. When filled, it is closed by holding down the flap and hooking the little ring over the hook as shown. When it is time to open it, the hook is slightly tilted forward and the lower flap falls down, thus allowing its contents to shower down onto a plate held to receive them.

This bag is hooked onto the back of the table. In the act of picking up the handkerchief, the little hook at the top is grasped through the handkerchief and the bag is drawn, by means of the hook, up into the sheltering folds of the handkerchief. A plate is then held beneath, a lady is asked to breathe on it, and the "shower of sweets" descends. While walking behind the table to hand the plate of sweets to the audience, the performer quickly drops the bag onto the servante, and the handkerchief is returned.

— The Vanishing Handkerchief —

Though simple, this is one of the prettiest sleight-of-hand feats in existence.

Use a fine, small silk handkerchief. Conceal a piece of the same silk rolled up into a ball and held between the joint of the thumb and the forefinger of the left hand. Roll up your sleeves and show that both hands are empty. Show the handkerchief and pass it around for inspection. Then take it between your hands and roll it up into a ball, which you pretend to pass to your left hand but really palm in your right. Let the small bit of silk in the left hand expand, so that the audience can see it and will be sure that the handkerchief is really there. While this is going on, drop the real handkerchief out of your right hand onto the servante. After a becoming amount of patter, join hands, roll the bit of silk into a tiny ball, and put it back in its original place. Then show both hands empty, the handkerchief gone. Cause the handkerchief to seem to reappear by allowing the small piece of silk to expand again, and finally to disappear, by vanishing the silk.

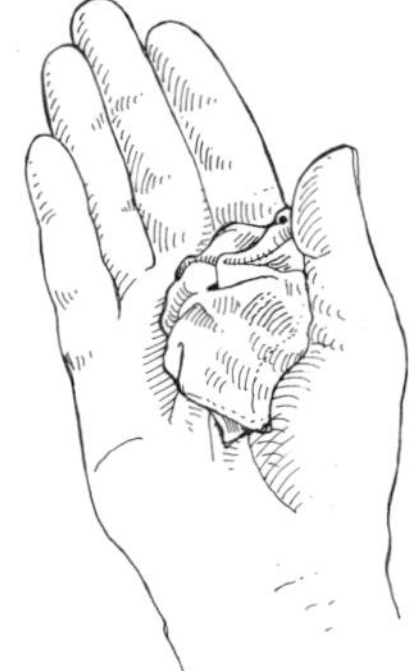

Palming the Handkerchief

— The Magic Knot —

This is a very amusing trick that consists of tying one knot with two ends of a handkerchief and pulling the ends, which only unties them again. Take the two diagonal corners of a handkerchief, one in each hand; throw the main part of the handkerchief over the wrist of the left hand; and tie the knot as shown in the illustration. Pull the ends quickly, allowing the loop over the left hand to slip free, and you will have the handkerchief without any knot.

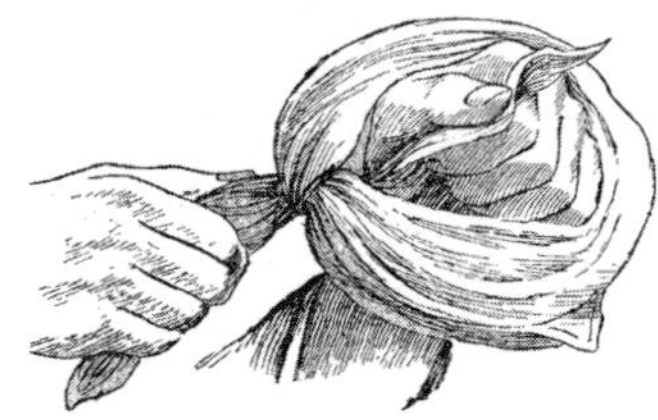

— The New Cylinders-and-Handkerchief Trick —

For this capital trick, you must provide yourself with two glass cylinders, each closed at one end. They may be procured from conjuring depots or constructed out of lamp chimneys (glass tubes that enclose a flame) by cementing glass disks to the ends of the chimneys. Preferably, they should have rounded bottoms, as depicted in the illustration.

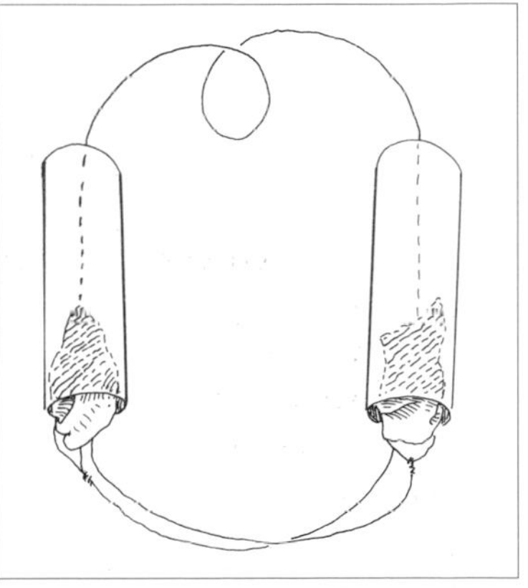

Figure 1

The effect of the trick is as follows: On your table are two cylinders. In front of each lies a handkerchief—one yellow and one red. Now pick up your left-hand yellow handkerchief and place it in the right-hand cylinder, and put the right-hand red handkerchief in the left-hand cylinder (*Figure 1*). Lay the cylinders on the table again and make a little speech about the rapidity with which articles sometimes change places, under the influence of atmospheric electricity. Pick up the cylinders, one in each hand, and move your hands quickly apart.

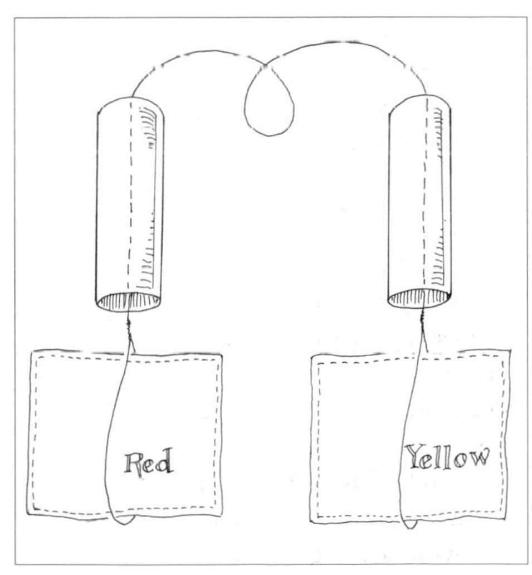

Figure 2

In the same moment, the handkerchiefs change places like a flash of lightning.

The secret of this very clever illusion will become apparent on consulting the diagram (*Figure 2*): The cylinders have little holes in the bottoms. A strong silk thread is run through them and looped about the handkerchiefs. A few trials will have to decide the proper length of this thread. The explanation of this feat is simplicity itself, but the effect is very bewildering on an audience.

— The Color-Changing Handkerchief —

The "Color-Changing Trick" is an exceedingly clever illusion, the requirements for which are as follows:

- Four white handkerchiefs
- One blue handkerchief
- One yellow handkerchief
- One red handkerchief
- A piece of very thin cardboard or stout cartridge paper, measuring 7 by 8 in. and gummed along one of its shorter edges.

The red handkerchief (*Figure 1*) is in reality two handkerchiefs sewn together at the edges. Between them, midway along one of the sides, a thin brass tube, *A,* is stitched by means of three or four minute holes in its upper end. This should be done in such a manner that the end is just level with the edge of the double handkerchief and therefore invisible when the handkerchief is spread out. The presence of the tube naturally creates a hiatus between the two handkerchiefs at the center. This is filled up by a gusset, *B, E, F, C,* of the same material. In the center of this is a hole, *D,* encircled by a rubber band. This allows it to be expanded to nearly the circumference of the tube, but normally contracts it to a very small size, so as to be scarcely noticeable. The two handkerchiefs are sewn together around the other three edges of the square, at points *B, E, F, C.* The intervening space forms an internal pocket accessible only through the tube, *A,* which is open at the bottom.

To prepare the handkerchief for use, it is first folded vertically in halves at the point where the tube is fixed. Beginning from the folded edge, the handkerchief is then rolled up, with the tube in the center.

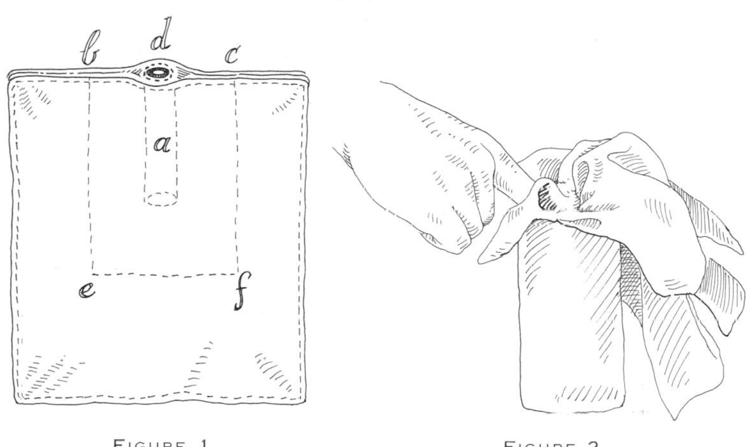

FIGURE 1
TWO HANKERCHIEFS SEWN TOGETHER

FIGURE 2
TUCKING IT INTO THE TUBE

Grasping the tube end with the right hand, the operator tucks the other portion of the handkerchief into the tube from the bottom, pushing it as far as it will go (*Figure 2*). This leaves a portion of the tube still unoccupied, and into this vacant space he packs first the yellow, then the blue, and last one of the white handkerchiefs. It will be found desirable to start with one corner, so that the opposite corner shall be the last portion to be inserted, and consequently the first to be squeezed out at a later stage of the trick. Each should be placed well home before another is introduced.

The double handkerchief thus prepared, and forming a compact roll only a trifle larger than the tube itself, is placed on the servante.

With the above arrangements having been duly made beforehand, the conjurer advances toward the audience, bringing forward the piece of cardboard and the three remaining white handkerchiefs. Placing the latter on his table, he calls attention to the former, and, beginning from one of its shorter sides rolls it into a cylinder, allowing it to expand again. The performer then places this on his table, letting the edge hang over the servante—on which rests the tube containing the handkerchiefs.

Showing his hands to be empty, he again picks up the bent cardboard, and with it the tube, using his right hand. Once more he rolls the cardboard into a cylinder, gradually making it smaller and smaller until it fits tightly over the roll, the latter resting with its upper end (the one with the hole, *D*) within ½ in. of one end of the cylinder. When matters have reached this point, he moistens the gummed edge of the cardboard with his tongue, then holds it down until there is no fear of its unrolling again.

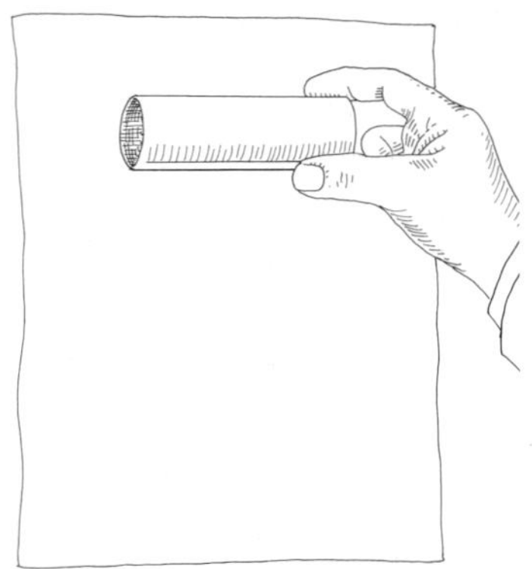

FIGURE 3
A PRETTY LITTLE SLEIGHT

It's worth digressing for a moment to describe a pretty little sleight that the performer will find useful, after he has picked up the paper with the tube behind it, to convince the spectators that he has nothing in his hands save the piece of paper. The paper is held by its upper right-hand corner, between the first and second fingers of the right hand. The tube is supported in a horizontal position (its upper edge, by the forefinger and the thumb, as shown in *Figure 3*). The performer takes the left-hand bottom corner between the first and second fingers of his left hand and turns the lower edge of the paper upward. When it has reached the position shown in *Figure 4,* the left thumb and forefinger seize the tube. The right hand moves away, and the original upper edge of the paper, now becoming the lower edge, is released. Both sides of the paper have thus been shown, and the paper and tube remain in the left hand, the transfer from hand to hand being a sort of tacit guarantee that there has been "no deception."

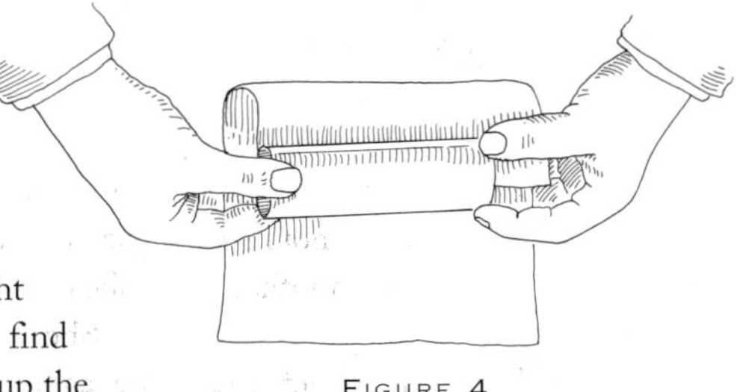

FIGURE 4
TRANSFERRING THE TUBE

Now, grasping the cylinder with the left hand (the end with the tube uppermost), he takes one of the white handkerchiefs and pushes it down, first with the fingers and then with the wand. It appears that the handkerchief is being pushed into an apparently empty cylinder, but in reality it is pushed through the hole, *D*, and into the tube. As the tube is already full, something must give way to make room for it. This something is naturally the white handkerchief that was the last to be packed into the opposite end of the tube, and which now begins to appear at the lower end of the cylinder. To the eyes of the spectators, this handkerchief is the same one they have just seen introduced at the top, and they are thereby convinced (if indeed they entertained any doubt on the subject) that the cylinder is empty. The oper ator must of course take care that the handkerchief shall not fall out at the bottom before the one at the top has entirely disappeared, or the inference would be in the contrary direction.

Taking the white handkerchief that has just appeared, the performer passes this in through the hole, *D*, remarking that he is going to change its color and turn it to blue. Accordingly, the blue handkerchief, which comes next in order in the tube, appears at the bottom of the cylinder. Laying this on the table, he takes another white handkerchief, presses it in at the top, and (apparently) produces it at the bottom, now colored yellow. Throwing the yellow handkerchief onto the table, he takes the remaining white handkerchief and pushes this likewise through *D*. This forces out the portion of the red handkerchief that was packed into the tube, and that now appears at the bottom of the cylinder.

This is the critical part of the trick, because the white handkerchief is naturally introduced at the top in "anyhow" fashion. Whereas the red one would, if permitted, come out rolled up. This fact, if observed, would tend to create a doubt as to their being, as the conjurer professes, the same. To avoid this, as soon as the white handkerchief is fairly within *D*, and the red handkerchief pushed down to within ½ in. or so of the bottom of the cylinder, the performer changes his procedure. Inserting a finger at the top of the cylinder, he gets hold of one of the upper corners of the handkerchief and holds it securely against the inner surface of the cylinder. Inserting the forefinger of the other hand, he now tears the cylinder open. As it falls, he gets hold of the opposite top corner of the handkerchief (the two lie, as will be remembered, one on the other). He draws them apart, spreads the handkerchief, shakes it out, and then catches it by the center, taking care that the hidden tube shall hang on the side remote from the spectators. Picking up the blue and yellow handkerchiefs, he transfers them to the same hand and, laying them on the table, proceeds with some other trick.

— Another Vanishing-Handkerchief Trick —

The necessary articles used in performing this trick are the handkerchief, the vanishing wand, a long piece of glass tubing about ½ in. shorter than the wand, and a paper tube closed at one end and covered with a cap at the other. The handkerchief rod, shown at *C* in the illustration, is concealed in the paper tube, *A,* before the performance. The glass tube, *B,* after being shown to be empty, is put into the paper tube, *A,* so that now the handkerchief rod is within it, unknown to the spectators. The handkerchief is then placed over the opening of the tube and pushed in by means of the wand. Doing this pushes the handkerchief and the rod into the wand, as shown in *D.* After the wand is removed, the cap is placed over the paper tube, and this is given to someone to hold. The command for the handkerchief to vanish is given, and it is found to be gone when the glass tube is taken out of the paper cover. This is a novel way of making a handkerchief vanish. It can be used in a great number of tricks and varied to suit the performer.

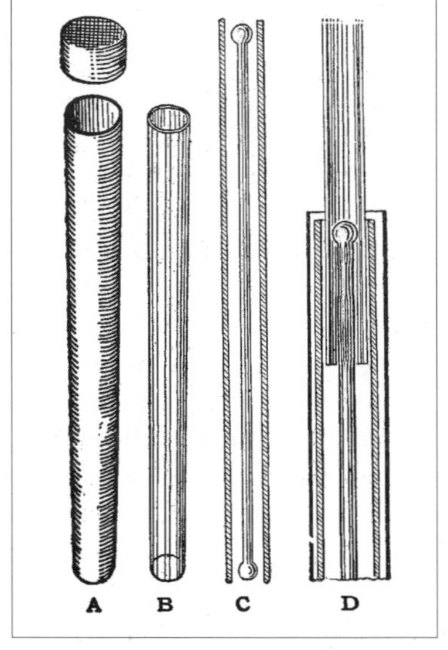

Tubes, Rods, and Wands

— A Decanter, Handkerchief, and Flag Combination —

The following is one of the prettiest, most charming, and most graceful openings to a magical performance that has ever been devised, and is due to Mr. Frederick S. Keating, who worked out the combination described below. It has never failed to incite the heartiest appreciation and applause.

The performer makes his entrance and, after showing his hands to be empty, produces a red, a white, and a blue handkerchief, with his fingers wide apart. He then picks up from his table two blue silk handkerchiefs, which he knots together and places in a glass decanter. This he stands on a small table, on the left-hand side of the stage, and it remains in full view of the audience throughout.

An unprepared piece of white paper is now shown and rolled into the shape of a tube, open at both ends. The performer pauses for a moment to explain that he will pass the red, white, and blue handkerchiefs through the tube, and as he does so, they will melt into the flag the three colors symbolize. So saying, he pushes into the lower end of the tube the red handkerchief, which is followed by the white one. But as the blue handkerchief, which is the next one, is inserted into the tube, it drops to the floor, through the apparent carelessness of the conjurer. The performer does not seem to notice this inexcusable carelessness; instead, with a triumphant smile, he pulls out from the opposite end of the tube what looks like an American flag—but without the stars of blue! Disconsolately he gazes at the unfortunate "fiasco," when suddenly he notices the blue handkerchief on the floor. He quickly picks it up and pushes both it and the incomplete flag back in the tube. Then, to the amazement of all, a complete American flag is pulled forth and laid on the table, and the paper is crumpled up and thrown to the audience!

The performer now exhibits a decanter, similar to the first, in which he places the American flag. "Now, watch me closely," says the magician, "for if you have sharp eyes, you will see the flag fly from this decanter into the one opposite, and knot itself between the two blue handkerchiefs that it contains!"

No sooner said than done! With a rapid upward sweep of his right hand, which is placed over the mouth of the decanter, the flag is seen instantly and visibly to vanish. Advancing toward the other decanter, the conjurer pulls out the two blue handkerchiefs that it contains—and, to the further amazement of the audience, the flag is now seen to be knotted between the two blue handkerchiefs.

The explanation of this extremely pretty and effective combination is as follows: First, as to the production of the handkerchiefs. One very good way to produce these is to have the handkerchiefs rolled up into a small package, tucked under the lower edge of the vest, and attached to a loop of black thread (the other end of which is fastened to the same side of the vest, beneath the arms). Now, by inserting the thumb in this loop and giving a sharp outward pull, the performer brings the handkerchiefs into his hand. All three can be produced in this manner at once if preferred, or they may be produced by any of the numerous other methods already described.

Having produced the handkerchiefs, the next step is to change them into the flag. An indispensable piece of apparatus is used for this purpose. This is known as a "handkerchief tube" (see illustration). It is a tube about 4 in. long and about ½ in. wide. A glance at the accompanying diagram will make its construction clear. A piece of tin or brass tubing of the required width is cut to the desired length. A series of tiny holes, about 1/16 in. apart, are punched around the center. A piece of strong black cloth is now made into a small bag about half the length of the tube, and this is sewn solidly to the holes in the tube. The result is that the bag can be pushed in either direction, as far as the end of the tube.

The preparation for the trick is as follows: place in one end of the tube the American flag first, then the incomplete flag. The tube, thus prepared, is placed on the back of the table—with the end containing the flags facing to the left. It is held in place by means of two pins or small pieces of bent wire, so that it rests just beneath the top of the table and behind it. The piece of paper lies on the table, the rear end just covering the tube.

The paper is now picked up, and with it the tube, and the paper is shown, apparently empty. The paper is now rolled around into a tube, and

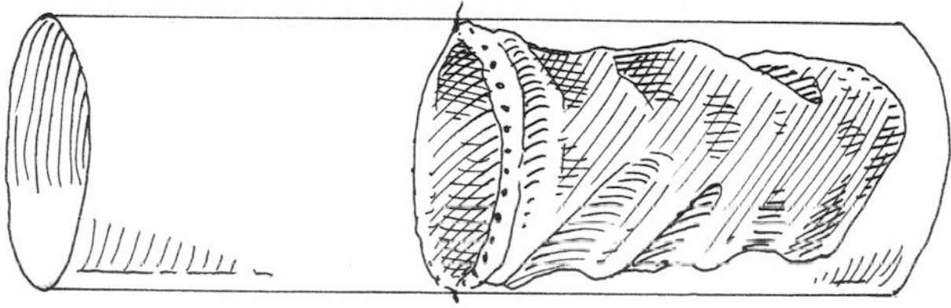

THE HANDKERCHIEF TUBE

the white and red handkerchiefs are pushed in, with the blue handkerchief being "accidentally" dropped. Needless to say, the first two handkerchiefs enter the actual tube, and, as they are pushed in, the upper flag at the other end is pushed out. The incomplete flag is now extracted and shown.

Your apparent "mistake" is now discovered, to the amusement of the audience. The blue handkerchief is picked up off the floor and pushed into the lower end of the tube, together with the incomplete flag. As these are forced in, the complete flag is pushed out. This is now extracted, and in the act of showing it, the tube (containing all the handkerchiefs and the incomplete flag) is allowed to slip from the paper onto the servante, by a slight relaxation of the fingers holding it through the paper tube. The latter may then be unrolled and shown to be empty.

Now for an explanation of the disappearance from the first decanter and the reappearance of the flag between the two blue silk handkerchiefs in the second decanter.

Over the middle finger of the right hand is a fine loop of catgut, the end of which continues up the right sleeve, across the shoulder, and under the vest, terminating in a loop just about even with the top of the left-hand trouser pocket. If this is properly arranged, it will not interfere with the first part of the trick, during which the loop remains over the finger.

As he explains what is about to happen, the performer casually slips the flag through the loop in the right hand, which is pushed into the decanter with the flag. Now, standing with his right hand toward the audience and holding the decanter by the neck with his right hand over the mouth, the performer, at the word "Three!" rapidly extends his right hand and arm out to their fullest extent, while at the same time the left hand catches the loop that comes from under the vest on that side and gives it a smart downward pull. In consequence of this, the flag will be drawn from the decanter and carried quickly and invisibly "up the sleeve"!

This is done so rapidly, however, that not even the sharpest eye can detect the movement. Of course, the left hand is not seen by the audience, being under the cover of his body.

As you place the decanter back on the table, quickly gather up with the left hand the loop of catgut (which has increased on that side) and stuff it into your trouser pocket. Although it remains there during the performance, it will not interfere in the least with your movements; in fact, it will hardly be noticed. Only in the first part of the trick will a little practice be required, so as to perform it smoothly, without the catgut interfering with your movements.

Great care must be taken not to extend the right hand too much, lest the left-hand loop be drawn up under the vest. This can be avoided, however, by sewing a hook to the top of the trousers, on that side, to which you attach a loop, until the time comes for its use.

Now for the knotting of the flag between the two silk handkerchiefs.

One of the handkerchiefs is prepared in the following manner: Sew, from the opposite corners, a triangular piece of the same material, thus making half the handkerchief a sort of triangular-shaped bag. Leave an opening about 1½ in. in the upper corner. To this same corner is knotted a duplicate flag. This flag is then pushed into the "bag" that is thus formed. Leave only a small tip extending. Because this is blue and the color of the handkerchief is also blue, it is not noticed. Now, when the other handkerchief is tied to the corner of the first, it is *really* tied to the corner of the flag, inside it. The result is that the three are now actually tied together, with the flag in the middle.

In placing the package into the decanter, insert the prepared handkerchief first and leave a corner of the real one protruding. That way, when you take it and give it a smart upward "flick" or jerk, the flag will be pulled from its hiding place in the fake handkerchief and will come out second. Care must be taken in knotting the handkerchiefs together not to show any of the flag.

— Untying-a-Knot Trick —

Tie a double knot in a silk handkerchief, as shown in the accompanying sketch, and tighten the last tie a little by slightly drawing the two upper ends. Then continue to tighten much more, pulling vigorously at the first corner of the handkerchief. Because this end belongs to the same corner, it cannot be pulled much without loosening the twisted line of the knot to become a straight line. The other corner forms a slipknot on the end, which can be drawn out without disturbing the form or apparent security of the knot, at the moment when you cover the knot with the unused part of the handkerchief.

When the trick is to be performed, tie two or three very hard knots that are tightly drawn and show your audience that they are not easy to untie. The slipknot, as described, then must be made in apparently the same way and untied with the thumb while the knot is within the folds of the handkerchief.

{CHAPTER 3}

SUPER-DUPER TRICKS

Eggs-actly

— Egg from a Handkerchief —

The handkerchief used in this trick should be large, say 18 in. square, and made of some stout, closely woven material. Fasten a black silk thread to the center of one of its edges. Fasten a blown egg at the other end of the thread. The string should be just long enough to allow the egg to hang down a fraction of an inch below the center of the handkerchief, from its edge, when the handkerchief is held by the corners of the side to which the thread is attached (*Figure 1*).

To show the handkerchief empty, palm the egg. With the same hand, grasp the right-hand corner of the handkerchief, and with the left hand grasp the left-hand corner. Then, by crossing the hands, show the other side. Thus, the back of the hand containing the egg will always be kept toward the audience. Once this is done, instantly drop the egg. To

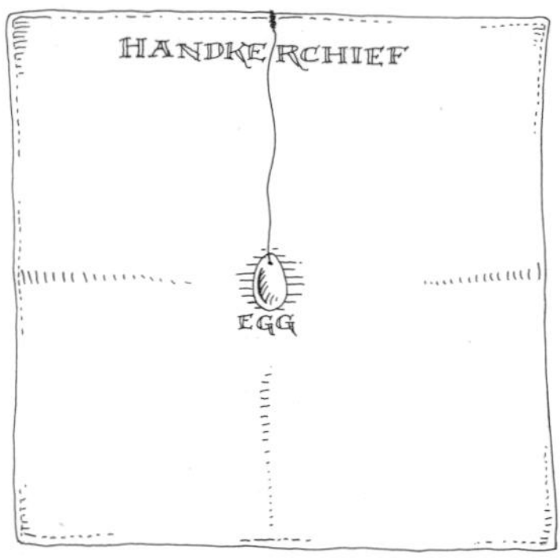

FIGURE 1
THE EGG HANGS
FROM THE STRING.

prevent it from swinging too far, and thus disclosing itself, quickly lower both hands and the handkerchief a little. The handkerchief may then be laid down anywhere, but care should always be taken to pick it up by the two corners of the side to which the egg is attached. The next step is to borrow a hat and a handkerchief from the audience. First, show that the hat is empty. Then place the borrowed handkerchief in the bottom to prevent breakage. The hat is then shown to contain only the carefully folded borrowed handkerchief. The previously prepared handkerchief is then folded in half by placing together the two corners you hold as you pick it up. Hold them in the right hand, and with the left fold it over once more. The handkerchief will thus form a sort of loose bag, open at both ends, with the still-unobserved egg hanging down inside it. Tilt the bag to a horizontal position (*Figure 2*) above the hat. If you now tilt it still more toward the hat, the egg will roll out of the right-hand

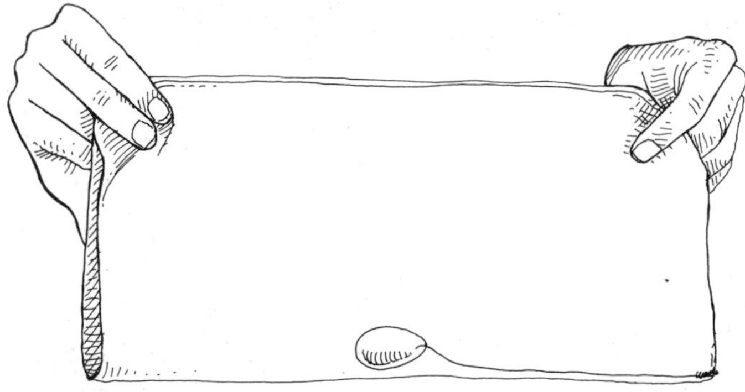

FIGURE 2
THE EGG HIDDEN INSIDE THE HANDKERCHIEF

end and fall into the hat, with the silk thread providing plenty of room for its fall. The audience thus sees one egg fall out of the apparently empty handkerchief into the hat.

As more than one egg is to be produced from the handkerchief, the next step—and perhaps the most difficult part of the trick—is to get the egg out of the hat without being observed. This may be accomplished in this way: The left hand drops the two corners it holds, and the handkerchief falls partially in front of the hat. The left hand then grasps one of the corners (until then held in the right hand), with the right hand retaining its hold on the other corner. When the handkerchief is raised, it will be in exactly the same position as before. The egg will be hanging down from the edge to the center of the handkerchief, and concealed by the latter, so that the trick may thus be repeated.

When this has been done some twelve or fifteen times, the audience begins to think that the hat must be full. The performer may pick it up with the pretense of great effort, then with effective byplay turn it upside down and exhibit it as being—empty!

— The Suspended Egg —

There's the trick of the suspended egg, shown in the illustration. Seemingly it defies natural laws by sinking halfway in a jar of water, then going no farther. The reason for this is that there are two liquids in the glass, one on top of the other. You must take care to prevent them from being mixed. The lower liquid is saturated salt water or brine, on which the egg will float

(rock salt is used, because it does not leave the water milky). The upper liquid is ordinary water, in which the egg will sink. After the salt water has been poured into the jar, a paper disk is placed on its surface and the water is added carefully with a spoon or siphon. Then the disk is removed, and the trick may be performed. You announce to the guests that you will cause the egg to submerge in this liquid and that it will come to rest about halfway down the jar. Someone is very likely to take issue with this, but when you drop the egg in the jar, that is just what happens.

— A Ring-and-Egg Trick —

This trick consists of borrowing a ring and wrapping it in a handkerchief from which it is made to disappear, only to be found inside an egg, selected from a number of blown eggs on a plate.

Before beginning the performance, place a small quantity of soft wax in the bottom of an egg cup; in addition, obtain a wedding ring and sew it into one corner of a handkerchief. After borrowing a ring from a member of the audience, pretend to wrap it in the center of the handkerchief. But instead, wrap up the one concealed in the corner, retaining the borrowed one in the hand. When getting the egg cup, secretly slip the borrowed ring into the wax in an upright position. An egg is then chosen by anyone in the audience. This is placed in the egg cup, with the ring in the bottom being pressed into the shell. The handkerchief is then shaken out to prove that the ring has vanished. Break the top of the shell with a buttonhook and fish out the ring.

— Make an Egg Stand Upright —

One of the first things to learn is how to make an egg stand upright. To make an unprepared egg do this is practically impossible, the yolk being relatively lighter than the white: as it is held suspended near the center, it is constantly shifting, the center of gravity also shifts, and the egg, of course, tumbles. To make it stand upright, it is therefore necessary to shake the egg violently so as to break the yolk and distribute it thoroughly among the white. The center of gravity is thus stabilized, and the egg may be balanced on its larger end.

Having mastered this, the performer offers a plate of eggs to the audience, inviting anyone to try to make one stand on its end. Meanwhile, he has a prepared egg palmed in his left hand. When all have failed to accomplish the desired result, he receives the plate of eggs back and, substituting his prepared egg for one that the audience has already tried, proceeds to make it stand upright on the table!

— The Spinning Egg —

Spinning an egg on end is also a trick that could hardly be introduced to an audience as a separate experiment, but which may be introduced to a small group—a "parlor audience"—with advantage. An egg, one of several in a tray, is offered to the spectators, and they are invited to try to spin it around like a top. They try but fail. The performer receives the egg back and proceeds to make it spin as long as he pleases.

The secret lies in the fact that the performer substitutes a hard-boiled egg, which may be spun around on its larger end, by the forefinger and thumb, and kept spinning by giving the tray a revolving motion on its own plane in an opposite direction to that of the egg.

Simple Stunners

— A Buttonhole Rose —

A "Buttonhole Rose" may be made to appear instantaneously in the following manner: The performer talks about the beauty of flowers in general, then suddenly asks, "Now, for instance, don't you think that a rose in my buttonhole would vastly improve my appearance? I shall try to make my magic wand bring me one." He then waves his wand toward the right, in order to attract the eyes of the spectators in that direction, and the rose suddenly appears in his buttonhole, where it holds its place for the rest of the evening.

The secret arrangement is as follows: A stemless artificial rose made of muslin is secured by a black silk rubber thread and arrested by a knot. It may be doubled, if necessary, to secure the required elasticity. The rose is held under the arm of the performer as he comes onstage. The cord to which it is attached then passes over the side of his chest, through the buttonhole, where it is attached to the rubber cord. This passes through a small eyelet sewn just underneath the buttonhole, on the inside of the coat, and then across the chest and around to the back, where it is secured to one of the right-hand buttons of the trouser waistband. The rubber band is just long enough to be taut when the rose is in the buttonhole. Thus, when the rose is under the outside armpit, the elastic is stretched. When the rose is released by elevating the left arm, the elastic contracts to its normal length, and the rose is snapped into place.

— The Birth of Flowers —

The "Birth of Flowers" is an old but interesting trick. The performer comes forward holding in his hand a small cardboard box that he says contains seeds of various flowers.

"Here, ladies and gentlemen, there is no need of earth, moisture, and time to cause the seed to germinate, the plant to spring up, and the flowers to bloom. Everything takes place instantaneously! A wave of my magic wand over these seeds, and lo! The wonder will be performed! A few seeds are in this little box, which I will cover for an instant, so that it shall not be disclosed how flowers are born. I now wave my wand and—

"But you are suspicious, I see, of this little box. Well, perhaps you are right. Very well; we will do without it! See, here is a goblet, all clear and transparent, so you may see that it is not prepared in any way. And now I shall borrow some gentleman's hat. Ah, thank you. Now, ladies and gentlemen, this hat is surely innocent of any preparation, and I place it for a moment over this little glass, and remove it quickly, and—what, no flowers here? Well, I am stupid. I forgot to sow the seeds. I will begin all over again. What flower do you want? A mignonette, a violet, a marigold—all are in here. Here is a seed of each kind, which I shall put into the glass. Now I cover the glass

FIGURE 1

for just a moment, count to three, and—see the magnificent bouquet!"

Finally, the trick is finished with the performer producing a number of small bouquets that he offers to the ladies.

As noted, the glass is first covered with a hat, and no flowers appear, at which the performer expresses his astonishment. But the moment when all eyes are focused on the glass to see the expected flowers, the hat is carelessly held near the edge of the table. While the audience is busy looking for the flowers, the performer's middle finger dips down and is inserted into the free end of a cardboard tube, whose other end keeps the flowers in place (*Figure 1*). Thus, the bouquet is safely snapped into the hat. This latter is then held aloft, while a few seeds are placed in the glass. When the hat is again placed over the glass, the bouquet appears (*Figure 2*). The performer then advances smilingly, as though he were going to return the hat, but he suddenly leans down toward his spectators and says: "What, you want some flowers? And you? And there are others who would like some too? Well, then, I will go and plant the rest of my seeds."

While all eyes have been turned to the bouquet, which has just appeared in the glass, the performer has introduced several small bouquets into the hat, and he now goes back, sprinkles the few seeds remaining into the hat, waves his wand, and produces and distributes the flowers.

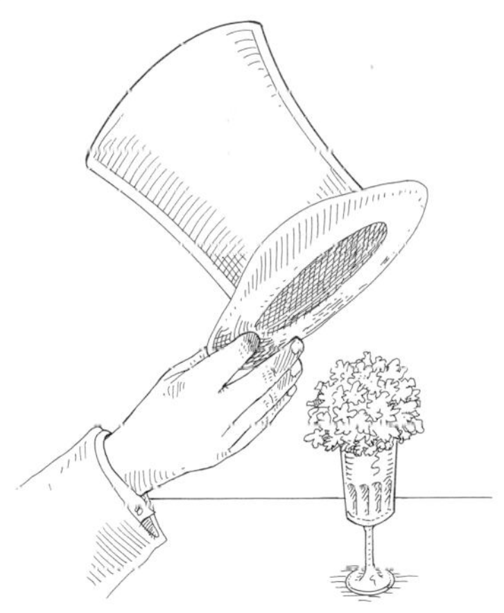

FIGURE 2

— The Soup Plate–and–Flower Trick —

The "Soup Plate–and–Flower Trick" is pretty and therefore effective, especially with the ladies. An ordinary soup plate is shown to be empty and waved in the air. Suddenly it is exhibited full of flowers, which may be distributed.

A rather flat bouquet, which may be concealed under one side of the coat under the arm, is fastened to a strong thread. The other end of this thread is passed through a hole drilled in the plate from the front, then attached to the lower button of the waistcoat. The plate is waved about, tapped with a wand, and so forth; the thread is invisible. The arm then shoots out, the bouquet is jerked from its resting place, and it appears on the plate. The flowers are clipped off and distributed among the audience.

— Removing a Key from a Double String —

Tie the ends of a 5 ft. long string together, making a double line on which a key is placed and the string held as shown by the dotted lines in the sketch. Turn the palms of your hands toward yourself, reach over with the little finger of the right hand, and take hold of the inside line near the left thumb. Reverse the operation and take hold of the inside line near the right thumb with the little finger of the left hand. You will then have the string as it appears in the sketch. Quickly let loose of the string with a little finger on one hand and a thumb on the other and pull the string taut. The key will drop from the string.

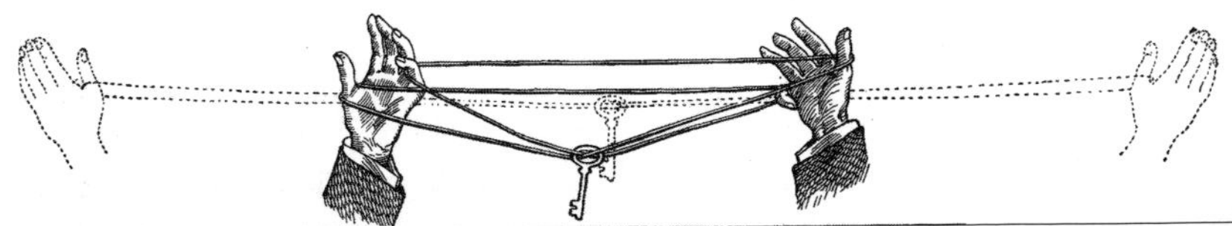

The key will drop from the string.

— A Finger-Trap Trick —

You can fool your friends with the little joker made to trap a finger. It consists of a piece of paper, about 6 in. wide and 12 or more in. long. To prepare the paper, cut two slots in one end as shown, then roll it up in tube form, beginning at the end with the cuts. Then fasten the end with glue. The inside diameter should be ½ in.

When the glue is dry, ask someone to push a finger into either end. This will be easy enough to do, but to remove the finger is a different matter. The end coils tend to pull out and hold the finger. If the tube is made of tough paper, it will stand considerable pull.

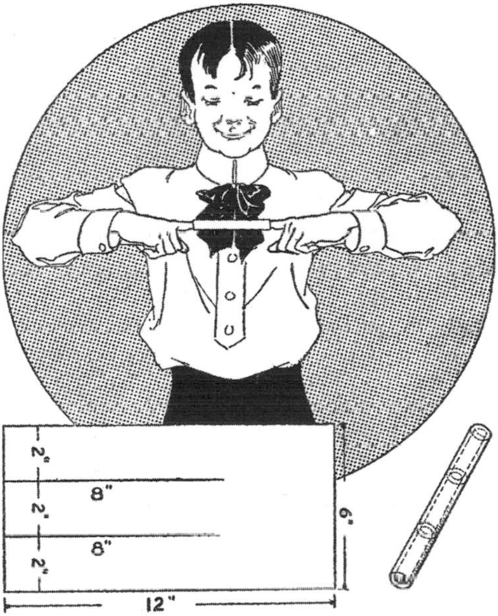

It is easy to insert a finger in the tube, but to get it out is almost impossible.

— Matter through Matter —

The effect of this puzzling little trick is as follows: The performer exhibits a solid glass bracelet that may be freely examined. He explains that it is made of glass, to show that no slits or anything like that are possible (which is a fact— the bracelet is indeed solid). The performer then requests a member of the audience to hold his hand securely (as though shaking hands); if desired, the two hands may even be bound together by means of tape or something similar. A borrowed handkerchief (which must be large) is now placed over the hands, so as to cover them both completely.

Now, taking the glass bracelet in the left hand, the magician places it under the handkerchief. He states that he is about to perform the experiment of passing "matter through matter" and will cause the ring to pass onto the wrist of his new assistant from the audience—"through his wrist." The assistant is cautioned not to let go of the magician's hand even for an instant while this is done. In a moment, the handkerchief is removed. The glass bracelet is now seen to be on the assistant's wrist—even though the hands are as tightly clasped and bound together as before. The bracelet may be examined again after being removed.

The explanation of this effective little trick is as follows: Two bracelets, exactly alike, are employed. One of them is concealed beneath the coat sleeve of the performer prior to the trick. Now, under cover of the handkerchief, this bracelet is worked down onto the magician's own hand, then over both hands onto the wrist of the assistant. The trick is now done; the second bracelet is simply removed under cover of the handkerchief and disposed of, while the audience is gazing, thunderstruck, at the bracelet on the assistant's wrist. The handkerchief may now be returned, and the second bracelet is taken off and passed around for examination.

— THE WALKING DOLL —

You can fashion a walking doll, using scissors and bond paper, that can be made to walk backward or forward on a tabletop to the wonderment of young and

old. Blow gently against the doll and it will "retreat." Hold your hand behind the doll, blow against your hand, and the doll walks toward you.

— The Color-Changing Paper Clips —

With a little manipulation, you can hook three different-colored paper clips together and then, turning your back for an instant, make any color jump to the center: red and then black and then back to white again.

The performer has an extra string of five clips in his vest pocket. He exhibits the original three-clip string and then, while turning around, sub stitutes the five-clip string. Any color called is easily gotten to the center by simply concealing the extra clips in the hands, as shown in the diagram.

At the conclusion of the trick, the three-clip string is substituted—"Here it is white again"—and everything can be handed out for examination.

Changing the color of the center clip

— THE FLYING THIMBLE —

This is a very simple little trick, being merely the passage of an ordinary thimble from the forefinger of one hand to the forefinger of the other, or to some other desired spot. Nevertheless, it may be presented with such variety that it becomes a valuable asset to any conjurer. The first qualification necessary is to become expert in palming the thimble with the thumb muscle, in the fork between the thumb and the rest of the hand. Thus, if the thimble is placed on the forefinger, the latter may be rapidly bent and the thimble deposited in its hiding place in the hand (see *Figure 1*). A reverse movement of the finger removes the thimble from the palm and again places it on the tip of the forefinger. This sleight is by no means difficult to acquire, and if performed with the arm in motion, the smaller movement of the finger is quite invisible. The only special precaution to be observed is to keep the hand in which the thimble is palmed with its back toward the audience.

There are many passes and variations that the performer may use, but space confines the description here to but a few. Some magicians begin with the hands in the position shown in *Figure 2,* the right hand having a thimble on the forefinger, and the left a thimble palmed in the fork of the thumb. The performer waves the right hand backward and

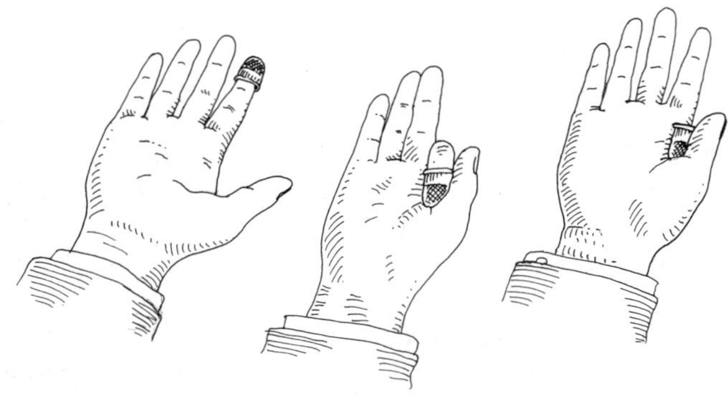

FIGURE 1
PALMING THE THIMBLE

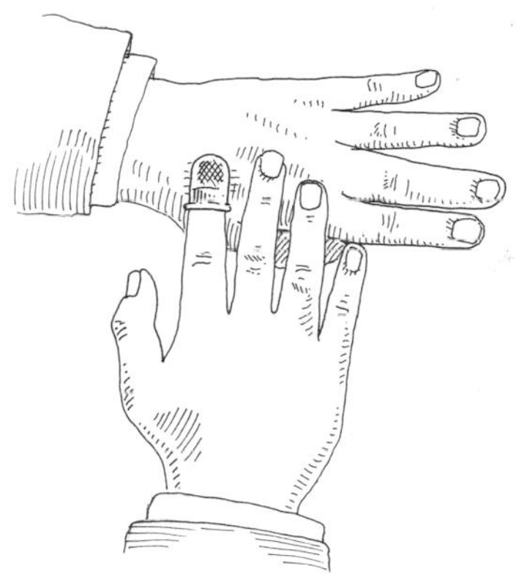

FIGURE 2
ANOTHER PALMING METHOD

forward alternately before and behind the other. As the fingers of the right hand vanish behind those of the left, he palms the visible thimble as described. At the same moment, the forefinger of the left hand is bent and the thimble appears on it, the effect for the spectators being that it has flown from one forefinger to the other.

A very good effect is to make the thimble presumably disappear through one part of the body and come out at another. Thus, the fore finger with the thimble on it may be put into the mouth, withdrawn with the thimble absent, and again produced from behind the head with the thimble in its place. Again, the thimble may apparently be put in one ear, then recovered from the other, and other passes of similar effect may be arranged by the amateur. When they are performed with ease and finish, they are both striking and amusing.

— THE TAMBOURINE TRICK —

Mr. Burlingame, in his "Tricks in Magic," gives the following pretty little experiment:

"The visible apparatus of this feat consists of two flanged rings of nickeled brass, 7 in. in diameter, as depicted in *Figure 1*; a piece of white paper about 14 in. square; and a pair of scissors. One ring, *A,* is of such a size as to fit easily over the other, *B.* Having submitted rings and paper for examination by the audience, the performer stands behind his table and explains that they are the materials for a tambourine. This he proceeds to construct by laying the sheet of paper on the top of ring *B,* then pressing ring *A* down over it, the thickness of the paper wedging the two rings together and causing them

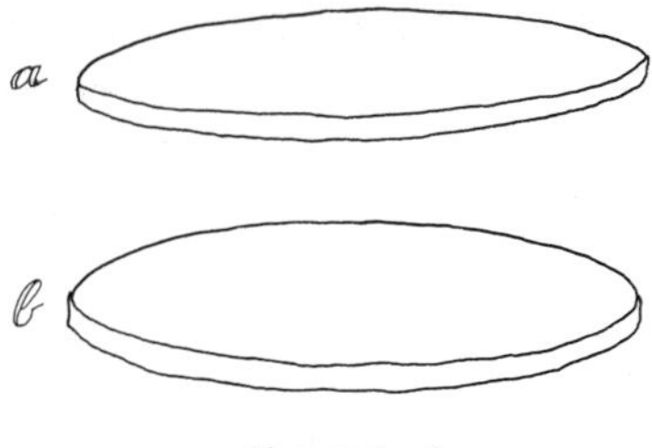

Figure 1
Two flanged rings

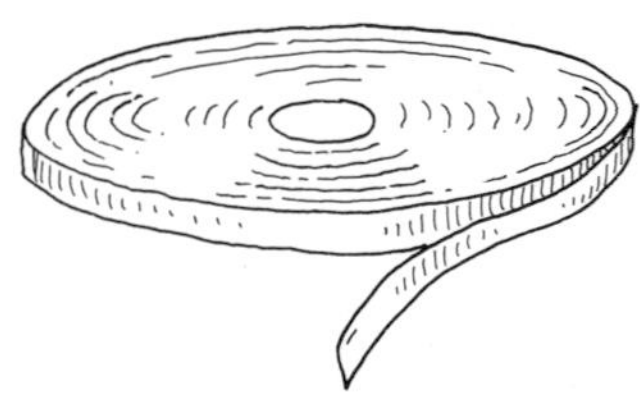

Figure 2
The coiled paper

to fit tightly. He uses the scissors to trim off the superfluous paper, and a neat tambourine is the result.

"His next proceeding is to thrust his wand through the paper from the outside and, from the hole thus formed, to draw yards upon yards of colored-paper ribbon, ½ in. wide, the quantity when all is drawn out being enough to fill a wheelbarrow.

"For greater rapidity in extraction, after he has got out half a dozen yards or so, he inserts his wand within the coils and draws out the remaining ribbon by quick circular sweeps of the arm. This brings out a couple of yards at a time, with very pretty effect.

"The secret lies in the fact that the paper produced is in the first instance coiled flat, after the manner of telegraphic paper (*Figure 2*). In this condition, a hundred yards or so occupies a very small space. When required for use, this coil is suspended

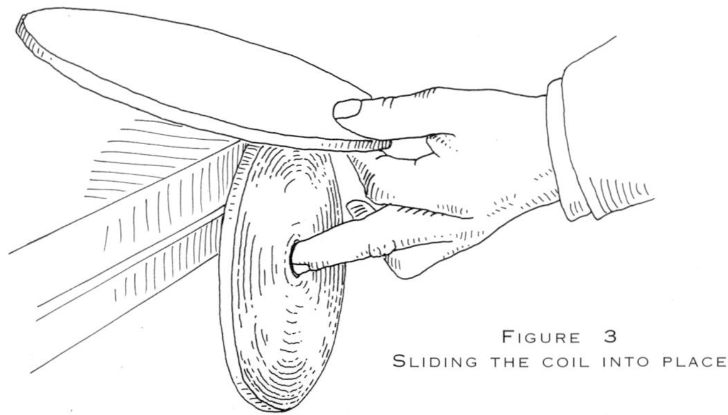

Figure 3
Sliding the coil into place

on a projecting pin against the back side of the performer's table, just below the top, in line with the spot on which the tambourine is to be formed. As soon as one ring has been placed over the other with the paper in between, the performer uses his right hand to pick up the scissors and trim off the superfluity. At the same time, the left hand grasps the tambourine between forefinger and thumb, drawing it backward off the table, as shown in *Figure 3*. Meanwhile, the middle finger, which is below the level of the tabletop, is inserted into the central opening of the coil and withdraws both together, the coil naturally settling itself within the inner circle of the tambourine. All difficulty is now over. The performer trims off the superfluity of margin as already described, makes the hole through the center, and produces the paper ribbon at leisure.

"Some performers dispense with the table and conceal the coil at the outset underneath their arm or inside the front of the vest.

"The tambourine can also be made in a small size, 4 in. in diameter, but in this shape the trick is much less effective."

— The Japanese Paper Trick —

The "Japanese Paper Trick" pleases an audience—as do most feats in which the performer introduces objects into one portion of his body and apparently produces them again from another!

A small piece of tissue paper is exhibited and slowly torn into eight strips. These the performer rolls up and places into his ear, before making them reappear from his mouth. He then puts them in a glass of water and stirs them around with a spoon, collecting them afterward in the bowl of the spoon. Then he places them in one hand; gently fanning this hand, he makes the papers appear fluttering in the air—perfectly dry.

Three pieces of tissue paper are necessary for the performance of this trick, two of which are torn into eight strips, and then two little packets are made of them. Stick an easily broken little band of tissue paper around one packet, and with a single drop of gum stick this to one side of an ordinary Japanese fan, at the fan's top edge. Position this fan lying on the table, with the side on which the paper is attached turned down. Just before commencing the trick, place the other packet in your mouth. Come forward and exhibit the third piece of tissue paper, then proceed to tear it up into eight strips, similar in appearance to the others torn up in advance. Roll this up in a small ball and either pretend to place it in your ear, palming it instead, or actually place it there and leave it. Then produce the previously torn-up pieces of paper from your mouth, one by one, and drop them into a glass containing water.

When all of them have been thus disposed of, take a spoon and stir them around, in order to wet them thoroughly. Then collect them in the bowl of the spoon and empty them into the left hand. Squeeze them up into a ball and retain them between the fingers. Take up the fan and advance toward the audience, saying a few appropriate remarks, and let the left hand naturally take hold of the top of the fan. Thus, while you are talking, the third packet is dislodged and rests on your left hand, which may easily break the tissue band. When the palm is opened and the hand is fanned, the papers will be sent fluttering in the air.

— The Multiplying Wand —

The performer comes forward with a plain, polished ebony conjuring wand of an ordinary pattern. He waves this about in the air—when it is suddenly seen to have multiplied into two wands. He then wraps one of these in a piece of newspaper, which he instantly crushes into a small mass in his hands, the wand having entirely disappeared.

It is needless to say that, to produce the above effect, two wands are necessary. One, however, is very different from what it is represented to be, being a mere shell of glazed black paper.

Prior to the commencement of the trick, the solid wand is encased in the shell, and in this condition it is brought onto the stage. In the course of waving it about, the performer allows the solid wand to slip out of the case, with a wand then being shown in each hand.

These can both be proved, in conjurer's logic, to be perfectly solid by adopting the following ruse: The performer strikes the table several times with the wand in the right hand, which is the solid one, after which it is apparently placed in the left hand, and the wand that was already there is treated in the same manner. When the two are both together in the left hand, however, the solid one is taken again, but the spectators, having seen no reason to suspect trickery, will suppose that the wands have actually changed places. The shell is then rolled up in a piece of paper and crushed in the hands, so that, to all appearances, that wand will have disappeared.

The trick may very well end here, or the vanished wand may be pro duced again. This may be done by having previously concealed a second solid wand in the leg of the trousers, in a pocket similar to that in which carpenters carry a rule. The two solid wands may then be struck together, proving their solidity beyond a doubt.

— The Phantom Wand —

This trick makes an admirable opening for a performance of magic: The magician takes his wand and proves its solidity by striking it on the table or the back of a chair. He then exhibits a long envelope, into which he pushes the wand, "to prove that there are no double compartments," and so on. This envelope should be just large enough to contain it. The wand is then removed and wrapped up in a piece of newspaper. The performer steps into the midst of the audience, explaining that he will cause the wand to leave his hands and fly from the newspaper, through space, into the paper envelope that he has just shown to be empty. With great solemnity, he then pronounces the mystical term "Hocus-pocus"—and like a flash, he crumples the paper and tears it into a dozen pieces, with the wand apparently having melted into thin air! The envelope is then handed to some member of the audience, who tears it open, and there is the magic wand—quite unaffected by its "wanderful" journey through space!

And now for the explanation: Around the wand was wrapped the previously described paper shell, painted to resemble the wand. When showing the envelope to be empty, instead of withdrawing the wand as he appeared to do, the performer simply allowed it to remain in the envelope and instead withdrew the shell. This, when wrapped in the newspaper, was readily crumpled along with it.

The best wand to use for this trick is a plain, polished stick. Some shiny black paper may be readily obtained from a stationery store, and, when rolled into the shape of a wand, it can hardly be distinguished from the real article. It is advisable to paint the inside black.

— A Paper Cornstalk —

Making a cornstalk sprout is another paper-tearing trick. First, roll six or seven double-sheeted newspapers lengthwise, one at a time, overlapping each sheet about 10 in. Then flatten the roll and, starting from the right side, tear down to a point a little beyond the middle. Do the same thing on the left, then rip out the center portion and discard it. Bend the leaves back, inserting a finger in the hole, and pull the stalk out in telescopic fashion.

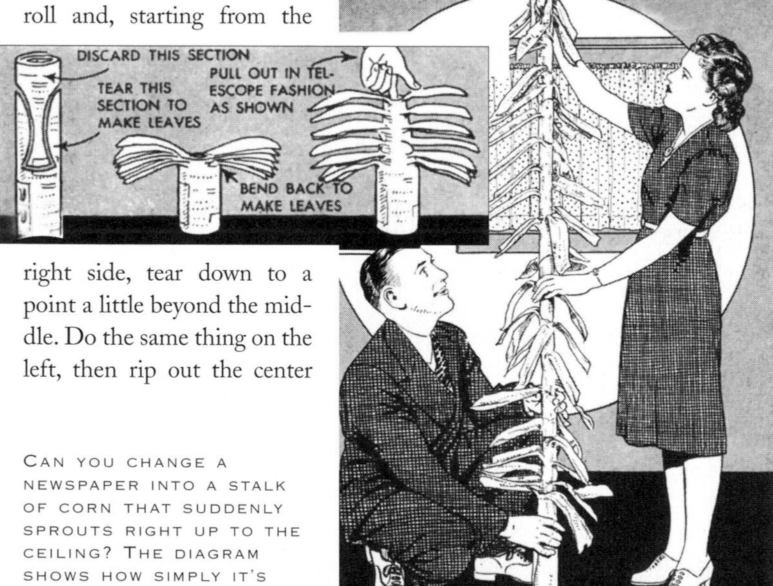

Can you change a newspaper into a stalk of corn that suddenly sprouts right up to the ceiling? The diagram shows how simply it's done.

— The Looped Cord —

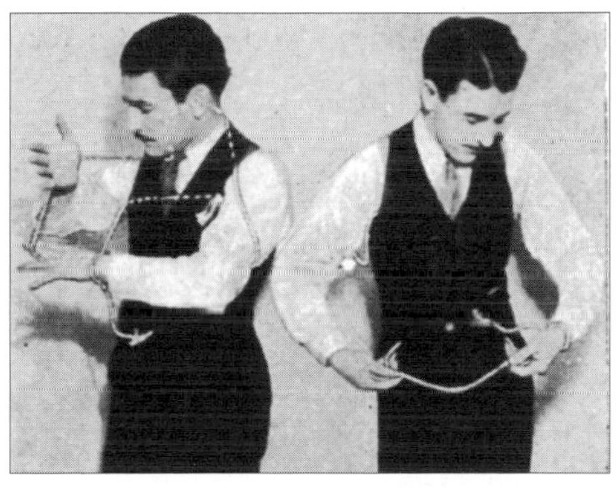

A length of soft cord is tied around the performer's left wrist. The free end is tied to his vest buttonhole. A second length is tied in a loop around the first. All knots are sealed with gummed tape and initialed. The photos show how the loop is brought up and through the vest, over the head, and down over the arm. Reaching up under the vest, you grab the cord and pull it free—all in a split second.

— The Buttonhole Trick —

This trick is performed with a small stick to which a loop is attached that is too small for the stick to pass through. Spread out the string and place it on each side of the buttonhole. Then draw the cloth around the hole through the string until it is far enough to pass the stick through the hole. Pull back the cloth, and you have the string looped in the hole with a hitch, the same as if the stick had been passed through the string.

Remove the stick by pulling up the loop as if you were passing the stick through it, putting the stick in the hole and leaving the string on the outside. Then spread the string, pulling up the cloth and passing the stick through the hole as before.

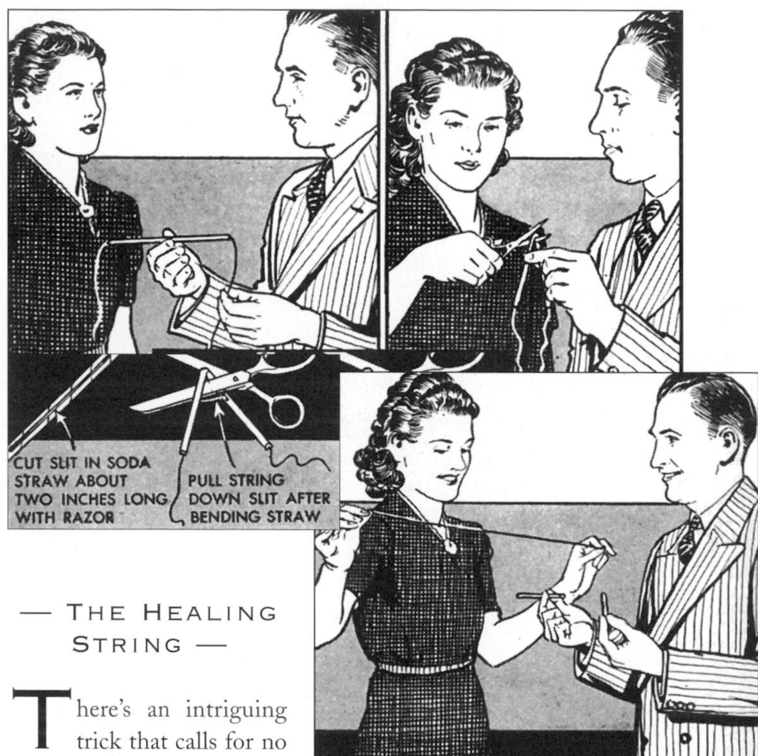

THE STRING IS THREADED THROUGH THE STRAW PREVIOUSLY PREPARED BY SLITTING; BEFORE LETTING A SPECTATOR CUT THE STRAW, IT IS BENT AND THE STRING IS SECRETLY PULLED OUT, SHIELDED BY FINGERS.

— The Healing String —

There's an intriguing trick that calls for no particular magic skill, yet ranks in interest ahead of many that do. Choose a soda straw—apparently at random—and through it thread a piece of string 18 in. long. Incidentally, the most practical way of accomplishing this is to suck the string through the straw as you would a drink. Then bend the straw in the center and ask someone in the group to cut it with scissors. After the cut is made and the straw pieces are separated, the audience discovers the string has been restored to one piece.

For this trick, some preparation is needed. The straw you seemingly select at random is one in which you have made a 1½ in. slit with a razor blade. In bending the straw, make sure the slit is underneath. Just before you invite a spectator to make the cut, pull the two ends of the string downward with the right hand so the string is through the slit. Your audience will not be any the wiser if you shield the string with your fingers.

— The Controlled Tube —

The controlled tube is a surefire hit. A magician shows a cardboard tube with a string passing through it. Holding one end of the string with his foot, he makes the tube rise or fall on the string at his command. When he hands the tube to someone in the audience, how ever, and suggests that that person do the same, the latter cannot do so.

Once again, the crux of the trick lies in the manner in which the tube is made. Inside it, about 1½ in. from the bottom, glue a small bead or ring. One end of the string is knotted to this, while the other goes through a suspended ring and out the top of the tube. A second string is attached to the suspended ring, the end of which the performer

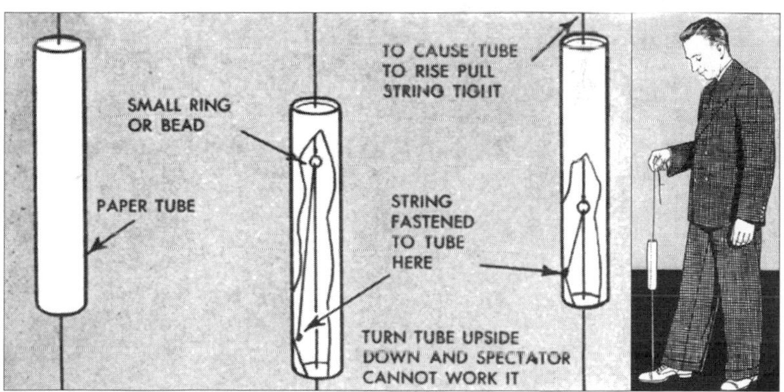

THE DIAGRAM ABOVE SHOWS HOW THE TUBE IS PREPARED FOR THE STUNT AT RIGHT, WHERE THE MAGICIAN MAKES THE TUBE MYSTERIOUSLY RISE AND FALL AT HIS COMMAND.

holds. When he wishes the tube to rise, he merely tightens the cord; if the tube is to go down, he keeps the string held limp. In handing the tube to the spectator, the magician turns it upside down. This causes the tube to dangle at the end of the cord, where it can't move.

— Jacob's Ladder —

Another paper-tearing trick is known as "Jacob's Ladder." The roll is prepared in the same manner as for the cornstalk trick. To prevent the roll from unwinding, place paper clips at either end and tear out the center portion. With this completed, bend the rolls downward and, grasping the paper strips between them, pull up the ladder.

At top left is the ladder of newspapers. They are rolled together with a 10 in. overlap as seen in the illustrations; the ends are clipped, the center section is torn out, the ends are bent down, and the ladder is pulled up.

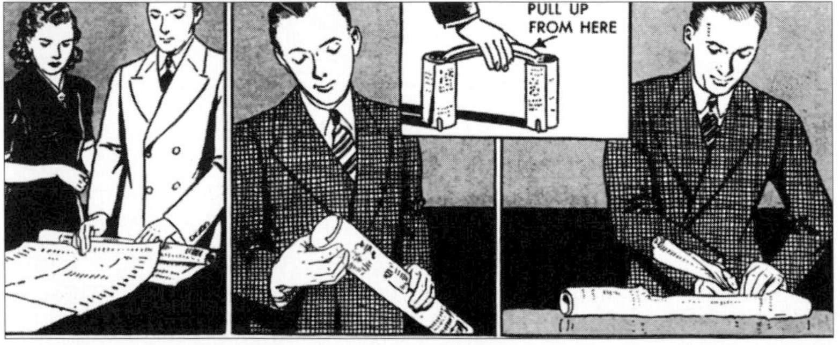

Perfect Party Tricks

— Walnut Shells and Pea —

This is an excellent table trick, and it can be performed at close quarters without fear of detection. The only articles required for the execution of this trick are three half walnut shells and a pea. The three shells are laid in a row on the table, with the pea placed under the center one. From this position it disappears, ultimately to be found under either of the end shells, at the will of the performer. The table used must be covered with a cloth of some kind.

The secret lies in the "pea," which is actually fashioned from a piece of India rubber. But unless it is closely inspected, it cannot be distinguished from the ordinary article. While performing the trick, the magician places the pea under the middle shell. Commencing with the one on the left, the shells are each in turn then pushed along the table about 3 in. When moving the middle one, the pea, owing to its nature and the concavity of the shell, will be found to work its way out. This is when it is instantly—and secretly—seized with the thumb and middle finger. This, however, cannot be suspected, as the hand retains a perfectly natural position while doing so. The third shell is then moved in a line with the other two.

The "pea" can now be caused to appear under either of the other shells at the performer's pleasure, all that is necessary being to leave it on the table immediately behind the shell, in the act of raising it up, so that it suddenly appears to have been under that shell.

— "Freeing Prisoners" Stunt for Your Party —

The performer ties the two wrists of a spectator with the two ends of a piece of string. Another string is then passed through the loop between the prisoner's hands, and the entertainer allows his own wrists to be bound in similar fashion. The object is to release the two strings, one from the other, so that the prisoners may go free. This is done by the performer bringing the center portion of his string up through the loop encircling one of the other person's wrists, over his hand, and down through the part of the loop at the back of his wrist. The strings will become disengaged, and the prisoners can go free, when the performer simply brings the middle part of the string over the other person's hand.

— A Simple Vanishing-Knife Trick —

The photos show, in order, a simple vanishing-knife trick. The napkin is draped over the conjurer's left arm, while the knife is held in the right hand (*Photo 1*). When the napkin is shaken open, the knife has vanished (*Photo 2*). The secret to the trick is revealed in *Photo 3:* while the knife is hidden behind the napkin, it is pushed up the left coat sleeve of the performer.

Photo 1

Photo 2

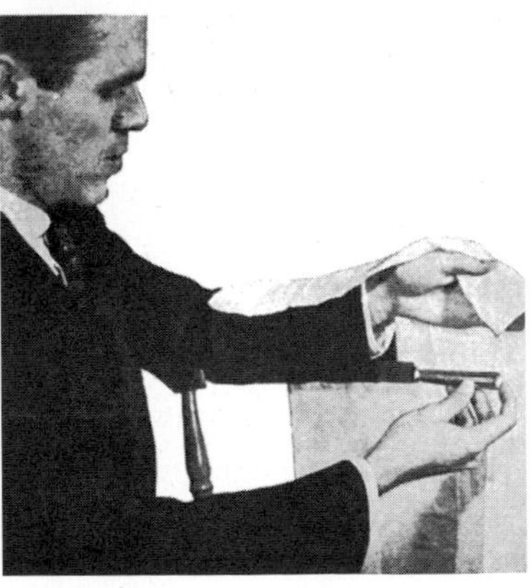

Photo 3

— Two Coins, One Hand —

The illustration shows two coins balanced on the edge of a tumbler opposite each other. The idea is to remove both coins at the same time, using only one hand. This is very simple once you know how. Just slide the coins toward each other by placing your thumb and finger over them as in the center detail, then bring both over the edge and together as indicated by the arrows in the third detail.

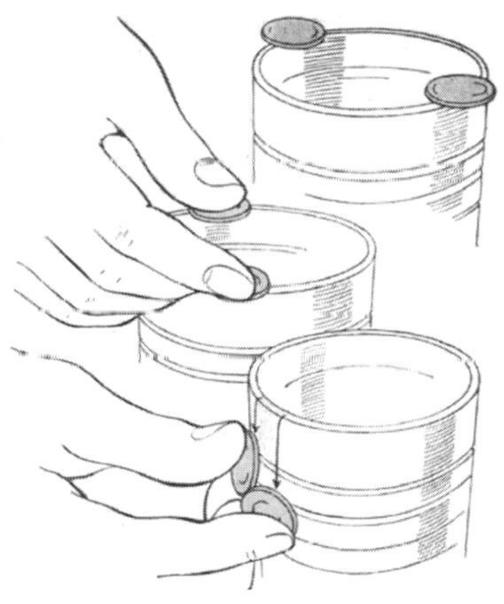

— The "Spirit Touch" —

This is more a joke than a trick, but it is amazing how much mystification can be caused by this simple sleight of hand, when it is well performed.

The performer asks his spectator to sit or stand in front of him. At the same time, he says: "Now I am going to place the first fingers of my two hands over your eyes. As I do so, please close the eyes, so that I can place them on your eyelids." Suiting the action to the word, the magician advances his two forefingers until they almost touch the eyes of the onlooker. The latter closes his eyes—and then, in the act of placing his fingers on the spectator's eyes, the conjurer quickly stretches out the first and second fingers of his left hand. It is these two fingers that cover the eyes of his onlooker. The latter now feels two fingers touching his eyes, which he takes to be both forefingers. He is correspondingly surprised when he receives a "spirit touch" on the back of his head—which, needless to say, is performed with the disengaged right hand of the performer.

The instant the magician has touched the sitter, he must bring back his right hand, stretch out that forefinger, and then slowly withdraw both hands as though drawing the two of them away from the sitter's face. The rapidity with which he does this "makes" the trick, because the sitter is apt to open his eyes as soon as he feels the touch, and if he sees the magician bringing back his right hand and arm, the effect of the trick is, needless to say, spoiled. Rightly performed, however, this will be found to mystify many people.

— The Paper Bridge —

Ask someone to lay a piece of writing paper across a couple of glass tumblers to support a third one partly filled with water. Of course, this seems impossible at first thought. The secret is to pleat the paper by folding it as in the illustration, and it will then sustain considerable weight before buckling. It's recommended to test the strength of the pleated paper by trying out the trick in advance, experimenting with filling the third tumbler to different levels and timing how long the paper holds it—as well as perhaps using unbreakable containers, at least for the tests.

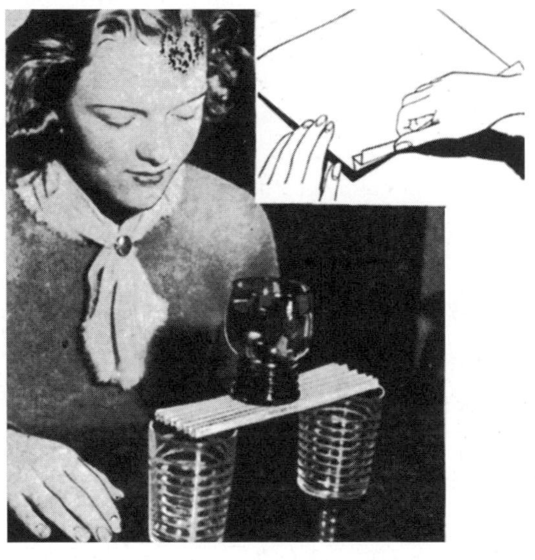

— The Wandering Penny —

For another coin trick, support a tumbler of water on two nickels under the base, with a penny placed midway between them. Ask someone to remove the penny without touching the glass or the nickels. The penny can't be blown out. For the trick, the setup is arranged squarely with the weave of the tablecloth. Then, by repeatedly scratching the cloth with your fingernail as in the photo, the penny will be coaxed out from under the glass.

— THE EMPTY-GLASS LIFT —

The next time you are having some refreshments with friends at a soda fountain, tell them you can lift an empty water glass without touching it. All you need is a bell-shaped glass and a soda straw. Before placing the straw inside the glass, bend it so it's a trifle larger than the diameter of the glass. Lift up on the straw lightly, and when the end comes in contact with the lip of the glass, a wedge will be formed sufficiently strong to sustain it. On your first attempt, pick out a landing spot for the glass that's softer than a soda-fountain marble top, in the event anything goes wrong.

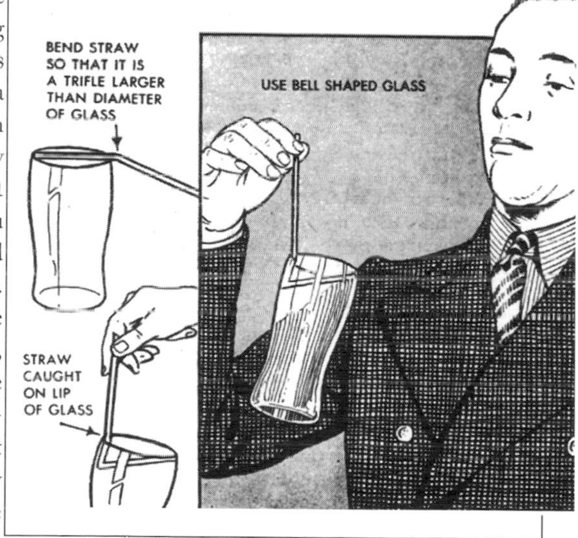

Big-Act Crowd Pleasers

— Making "Spirits" Play a Violin —

A very pretty trick that can be worked in your own parlor will produce as much sensation as a fake "medium." To all appearances, a violin, mandolin, or guitar placed on a table will begin to produce music simply through stamping the foot and making a few passes with the hand. The music will not sound natural, but weird and distant.

THE MUSIC PRODUCED BY THE PHONOGRAPH IS TRANSMITTED TO THE VIOLIN ON THE SECOND FLOOR BY THE AID OF A LONG STICK.

The trick is done by placing the end of a small stick on a music box in the basement of the house and allowing the other end to pass up through the floor and tabletop, so that it will project about 1/16 in. The stick may be placed by the side of, behind, or through the center of the table leg. Be careful not to have any obstruction in the way of the stick. The instrument is placed sideways on the protruding end of the stick. The "fake" work of invoking the "spirit" is performed and ended by stamping the foot, which signals the operator in the basement to start the machine. The violin seemingly produces music without anyone touching it.

So impressive are the results that many people really think the spirits of the departed are playing the violin with unseen hands. The music is transmitted through the stick from the music box to the violin.

— A Sack Trick —

The magician appears, accompanied by his assistant. He has a sack similar to a meal bag, only on a large scale. The upper end of this bag is shown in *Figure 1,* with the rope laced in the cloth. He then selects several people from the audience as a committee to examine the sack to see that there is absolutely no deception whatever in its makeup. When they are satisfied that the sack is all right, the magician places his assistant inside it. Drawing the bag around him, the assistant allows the committee to tie him up with as many knots as they choose to make, as shown in *Figure 2.*

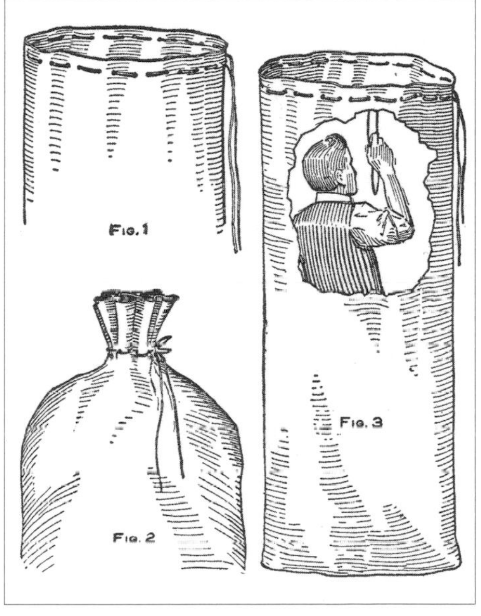

The sack trick—
holding the rope inside the bag

The bag with its occupant is placed inside a small cabinet, which the committee surrounds to see that there is no outside help. The magician then takes his watch and shows the audience that in less than thirty seconds, his assistant will emerge from the cabinet with the sack in his hand. This he does, after which the sack is again examined and found to be the same as when it was first seen.

The solution is that when the assistant enters the bag, he pulls in about 15 in. of the rope and holds it, as shown in *Figure 3,* while the committee is tying him up. As soon as he is in the cabinet, he merely lets out the slack, thus making enough room for his body to pass through. When he is out of the bag, he quickly unties the knots and then steps from his cabinet.

— An Electric Dancer —

The modification of the well-known mechanical dancer shown in the illustration is based on the principle of the electric bell. While the amusing antics of the mechanical dancer are controlled by the hand, the mannequin shown is actuated by the electromagnet.

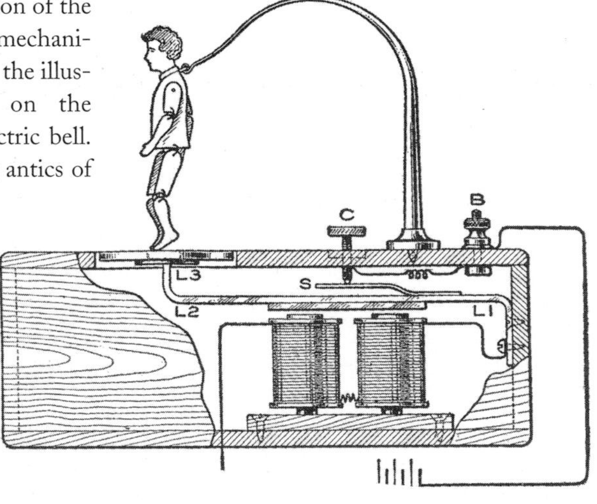

When the contact is made, the figure dances.

The mechanism is contained in a box. It consists of an electromagnet with a soft-iron armature caried by a spring. A wire from the battery goes to the magnet. The other terminal of the magnet connects with the armature springat *L1.* The spring is bent at a right angle at its other end, *L2,* and carries a platform, *L3,* strengthened by a smaller disk underneath. The dancer performs on this platform.

A contact spring, *S,* is carried by the armature spring, *A.* A contact screw, *C,* is adjustable in its contact with the spring, *S.* A wire runs from the contact screw, *C,* to the binding post, *B,* to which the other battery wire is connected.

The current keeps the platform in constant vibration, causing the figure to "dance." By means of the screw, *C,* the action of the current may be varied, and the "dancing" will vary correspondingly.

The figure is made of wood with very loose joints and suspended so the feet barely touch the platform.

— Goldfish Travel from Bowl to Bowl —

An interesting and entertaining arrangement—permitting goldfish in one bowl to travel to another—is created as shown in the drawing. An extra fishbowl is provided and filled with water to the same height as the one containing the fish. Then a piece of glass tube, of large diameter, is made into an elongated "U," by heating it where the bends are to be and slowly bending it. After it has cooled, this U-shaped tube is filled with water, and one end is placed in each bowl. The water will remain in the glass tube, even though the tube is above the level of the two bowls, so long as the water in both is kept above the ends of the tube.

An arrangement that permits goldfish in one bowl to swim to another through a glass tube

— Removing Thirty-six Cannonballs from a Handbag —

The magician produces a small handbag and informs the audience that he has filled it with twenty-pound cannonballs. He opens up the bag and takes out a ball, which he passes around the audience. The ball

Cannonballs made of spring wire

is examined and found to be the genuine article. He makes a few passes with the wand and produces another ball, and so on, until thirty-six of them lie on the floor.

In reality, the first ball—the one examined—is the real cannonball. The others are spiral-spherical springs covered with black cloth (*Figure 1*). These balls can be pressed together in flat disks and put in the bag (*Figure 2*) without taking up any great amount of space. When the spring is released, it will fill out the black cloth to represent a cannonball that cannot be distinguished from the real article.

— The Die-and-Box Trick —

The "Die-and-Box Trick," so often performed on the stage, is a very interesting and mystifying one. The apparatus, however, is simple. It consists of a box, die, a piece of tin in the form of three adjacent sides of the die, and a hat. The die and box are constructed entirely of wood, ⅛ in. thick, and the piece of tin can be cut from any large coffee can. The box is closed by four doors, as shown in *Figure 1,* two of which are 2¾ in. square, and the others are 3⅛ by 3¼ in. The first two are the front doors and are preferably hinged with cloth to the two uprights, *A* and *B.* Small pieces of tin are fastened on the doors at *C* and *D,* to provide a means to open them. The other doors are placed on top and are hinged to the back, as shown.

The die is 3 in. square on all sides and is constructed of two pieces 3 in. square, two pieces 2¾ by 3 in., and two pieces 2¾ in. square. These are fastened together with ½ in. brads. The tin, forming the false die, is cut out as shown in *Figure 2,* then bent on the dotted lines and soldered together on the joint formed by the two edges *E* and *F.* All parts should be painted a dull black with white spots on the die and false die.

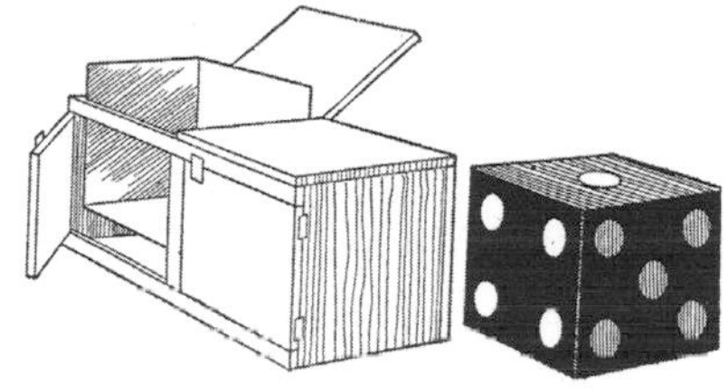

WITH THE FALSE DIE IN PLACE IT APPEARS AS IF THE BOX WERE EMPTY.

The trick is performed as follows: Procure a hat from someone in the audience and place in it the die with the tin false die covering three sides of a block, at the same time telling the audience that the block will be caused to pass from the hat into the box, the latter being placed some distance away. Inform the audience that it would be more difficult for the die to pass from the box into the hat. Remove the tin piece from the hat and leave the die, holding the surfaces of the false die toward the audience. This will give the impression that the die has been removed.

Set the hat on the table, above the level of the eyes of the audience. With the back of the box toward the audience, open one top door and insert the tin piece in the right-hand compartment so that one side touches the back, another the side, and the other the bottom of the box. Close the door and open the two doors of the opposite compartment, which, when shown, will appear to be empty. Tilt the box to this side and open the doors of the side opposite

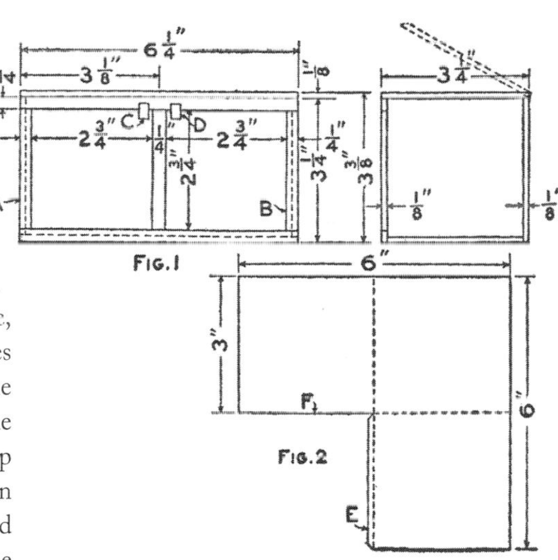

THE BOX (FIG. 1) WITH DOORS ON ONE SIDE AND THE TOP, AND THE FALSE-DIE PATTERN (FIG. 2)

to the one just opened, which, of course, will be empty. This should be done several times until someone asks that all doors be opened at the same time. After a few more reversals and openings as given, open all doors and show the box to be empty; then take the die from the hat.

TIME *to* AMAZE

— THE MAGIC CLOCK HAND —

The hand, or pointer, is the only working part needed to perform this trick. A clock face can be drawn on any piece of white paper, and a pin, on which the hand will revolve, is stuck in its center. The hand, *A,* is cut from a piece of sheet brass and may be in any form or design desired. It must, however, balance perfectly on the axle that passes through a ¼ in. hole in the center, or else the magic part will fail. The illustration at far right shows a good design with dimensions that will cause it to balance well. However, this can be adjusted either by removing some metal from the end that is heavier, using a file or tinsmith's

A NUMBER IS MENTIONED AND THE PERFORMER GIVES THE WASHERS A TWIST TO SET THE CONCEALED WEIGHT SO THAT THE HAND WHEN HUNG ON THE DIAL WILL BE DRAWN TO POINT OUT THE NUMBER SELECTED.

snips (metal shears), or by sticking a bit of solder to the lighter end.

A disk, *B,* is cut from a piece of sheet brass, 1⅛ in. in diameter. Twelve 3/32 in. holes are drilled at an equal distance apart near the edge, and a ¼ in. hole is drilled in its center. This disk is soldered to the hand where both ¼ in. holes will coincide. It is necessary to procure two washers, *C* and *D,* which are embossed—raised—in the center and about 1¼ in. in diameter. These can be purchased from a dealer in curtain rods; they are the washers used on the ends of the rods. A careful mechanic can raise the center portion of a brass disk by beating it over a hole with a ball-peen hammer.

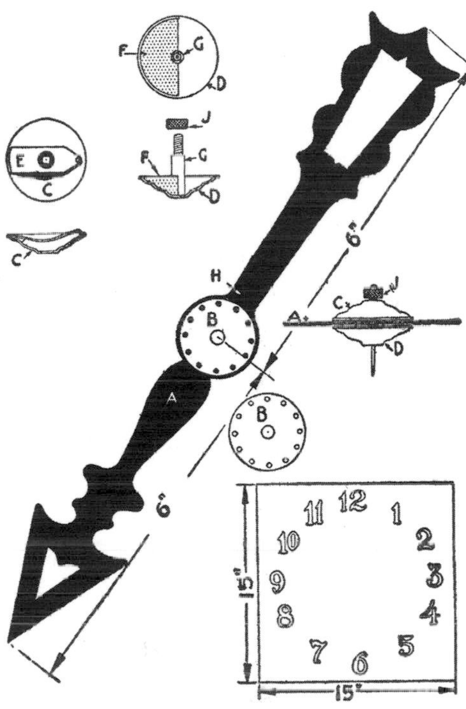

THE DESIGN OF A HAND THAT WILL BALANCE WELL, AND THE PARTS FOR ITS AXLE

One of the washers, *C,* has a spring, *E,* soldered at one end, and the other carries a small projection that will engage the holes in the disk, *B.* The projection can be made by driving the metal out with a center punch set on the opposite side.

The other washer, *D,* is provided with a lead weight, *F,* and a ¼ in. stud, *G,* is soldered in the center. The stud has a 1/16 in. hole drilled through its center for the pin axle. The weight is made by filling the washer with melted metal, which when cold is removed and sawn in two. One piece is then stuck in the washer with shellac. The stud is ⅞ in. long, with the upper part about ¼ in. long, filed, or turned down, smaller and threaded. Just below the thread, or on the shoulder, the body is filed square to fit a square hole filed in the face of washer *C*, carrying the spring. This square hole and stud end are necessary for both washers to turn together.

The dial can be made of a piece of thick cardboard or thin wood, with the numbers 1 to 12 painted on like a clock face. A pin 1/16 in. in diameter, or an ordinary large pin, is run through the center so that it will project on the face side, on which the hand is to revolve.

Washer *D*, with the weight, is placed on the rear side of the hand, with the fixed stud running through the hole in the center of the hand. Then washer *C* is placed on the square part of the stud, and the nut, *J*—which should have a round, knurled edge—is turned on the threads. This will cause the projection on the spring, *E*, to engage one of the small holes on the disk, *B*. In turning the two washers, *C* and D, with the thumb and forefinger of the right hand, the projection snapping into the holes of the disk, *B*, can be felt. The hand is placed on the pin of the clock face, and the washers are turned so that the weight will make it point to 12. Scratch a mark on the hand at *H*. Also mark a line on the front washer at this point. These lines are necessary, as they enable the performer to know how many holes to snap the spring over to have the hand point at any desired number.

By reversing the hand, it will point to a different number; for instance, if set for 8 and put on the pin backward, it will point to 4, and so on with other settings. The dial can be held in the hand, hung on a stand, or fastened to a wall. And with different numbering, it can be used for the day of the week, time of day, cards selected, and so on. The audience can call for any number on the clock face, and the setting of the disks is an easy matter while holding the hand, or pointer, in the hands, so that it cannot be detected.

— The Watch That Obeys —

The following is a very amusing trick, and it is always greeted with gales of laughter. The performer borrows a watch, holds it up to his ear, and, nodding his head reassuringly, announces that it is running fine. He then holds it to the ear of one of the audience, so that his judgment may be confirmed, and the spectator declares that the watch has stopped. "Oh, you must be mistaken," you cry, and offer it to another person to listen to. This person declares that it is still going. Offer it to other members of the audience, with each one contradicting the one before.

The secret lies in a lodestone, which you have palmed in your right hand. When this is applied to a good watch (and it is wise to see that the one you borrow is a good watch and therefore has delicate works), the attraction will stop the movement, and the person to whose ear it is applied will declare it has stopped. When the lodestone is removed, the watch will commence ticking again (or a slight shake will make it do so), the next person will declare it is going, and so on.

— A Mystifying Watch Trick —

Borrow a watch from one of the audience and allow the owner to place it in the box, as shown in *Figure 1.* This box should be about 3 in. long, 4 in. wide, and 2½ in. deep, says the *Scientific American.* It should be provided with a hinged cover, *M,* with a lock, *N.* The tricky part of this box is the side *S,* which is pivoted at *T* by driving two short nails into it. One is driven through the front side and the other through the back, so that when the side S is pushed in at the top, it swings around as shown in *Figure 1* and allows the watch to slide out into the performer's hand. The side *S* should fit tightly when closed, so that the box may be examined without betraying the secret. As the side *S* extends down to the bottom of the box, it facilitates the use of the fingers in pulling outward at the lower part while the thumb is pressing inward at the top part. The side of the box opposite the side S should be built up in the same way, but not pivoted.

Use a flat-bottom tumbler, *A* , containing an inner cone, *B,* for the reproduction of the watch (*Figure 2*). The cone is made of cardboard pasted together so that it fits snugly inside the tumbler. The cone is closed except at the bottom; then bran is pasted on the outside surfaces to make the tumbler appear as if it is filled with bran when it is in place.

Place the tumbler with the cone inside on a table somewhat in the background. Put some loose bran on top of the cone and allow the cork, attached as shown in *B* (see *Figure 2*), to hang down on the outside of the tumbler, away from the audience. A large handkerchief should be laid beside the tumbler.

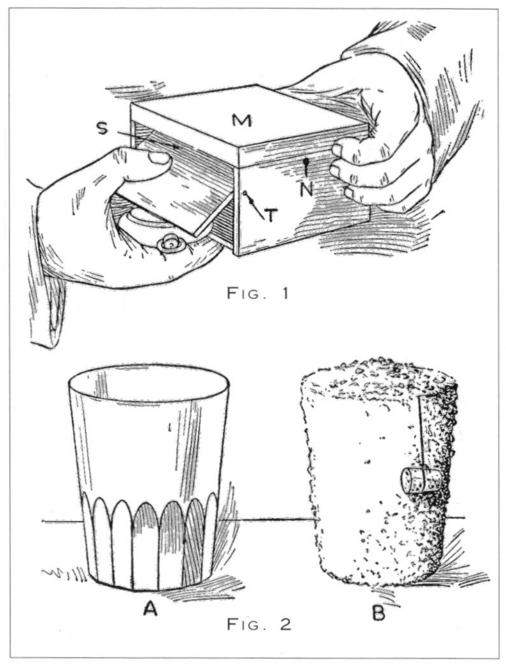

Parts for the watch trick

After the watch has been placed in the box (*Figure 1*), the performer takes the box in his left hand. While in the act of locking it with his right hand, he secures possession of the watch, as previously explained. Tossing the key to the owner of the watch, the performer places the box on a chair or table near the audience and then, with the watch securely palmed, walks back to get the tumbler. Standing directly in front of the tumbler with his back toward the audience, the performer quickly raises the cone with his right hand, lays the watch in the bottom of the tumbler, and replaces the cone.

The loaded tumbler and the handkerchief are then brought forward, and the former is placed in full view of the audience, with the cork hanging down behind it. The performer calls attention to the tumbler being full of bran and picks up some of it from the top to substantiate his statement. He then spreads the handkerchief over the tumbler, commanding the watch to pass from the box into the tumbler and the bran to disappear.

The box is then handed to the owner of the watch so that he may unlock it with the key he holds. As soon as the box is found to be empty, the performer grasps the handkerchief spread over the tumbler, as well as the cork tied to the cone. Raising the handkerchief, he carries up the cone within it, leaving the watch in the bottom to be returned to its owner.

PLAYING *with* FIRE

— WHAT, NO MATCHES? —

This stunt takes a bit longer telling than doing. You see, a man wanted a box of matches, so he walked into a cigar store. (Extend the left hand to indicate the store, and place a penny box of matches on it.) There was nobody in the store (lift the matchbox and show that the hand is empty, both back and palm), but a full box of matches rested on the counter (open the box and show it to be full). What did the man do? He quietly lifted the matches, placed them in his pocket, and walked out. (Pick up the matchbox with the right hand and place it in the right trouser pocket, then close the left hand.) The man was hardly out of the shop when the proprietor came running and demanded his money. (Extend

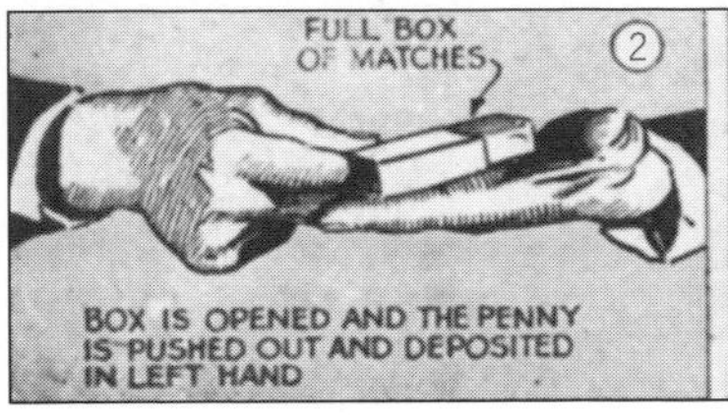

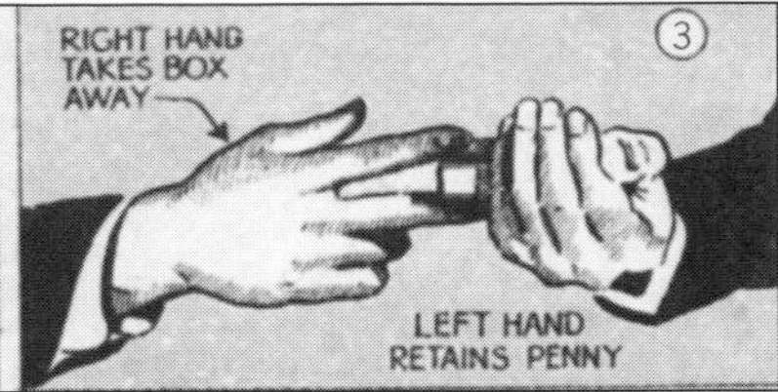

Steps in the matchbox-and-penny trick

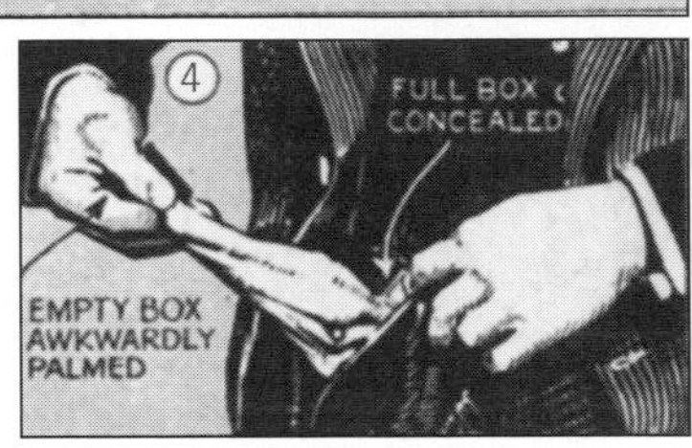

the forefinger of the left hand and tap across the table.)

The man told the proprietor that he paid for the matches. So they returned to the store. Sure enough, the payment for the matches rested on the counter. (Open the left hand—and there's a penny.) Of course, the man got the matches back again, but when he opened the box to get a light, the matchbox, which a moment before had been shown full, is now empty! (Open the box again and show it to be empty.)

Here's how the trick is worked: First, you need two boxes, exactly alike. One of these, an empty box, is in your right trouser pocket at the start of the trick. The second one, a full box, is prepared by cutting a little projection on the underside of the drawer, as shown in *Figure 1,* so that if you slip a penny between the cover and the drawer and close the box, the coin will be pushed out again when the box is opened. This opening of the box, as already described, happens on your left hand, as shown in *Figure 2.* When you close the box, do it as shown in *Figure 3,* closing the left hand at the same time and retaining the penny.

Place the full box in your pocket and, while giving the patter, quietly push it up into the extreme top corner of the pocket. Awkwardly palm the empty box and show your pocket empty. In *Figure 4,* the edge of the pocket is pulled back to show the position of the concealed full box. This, of course, is ordinarily well out of sight. The rest of the trick is as described in the patter.

— A Matchbox Trick —

All that is required to perform this trick is a box of safety matches. Four matches are removed and three of them arranged as shown in the sketch. The performer tells his friends that he will light the fourth match and set the cross match on fire in the center, then asks which match of the standing ones will light first. Most people will not stop to think, but will guess either one or the other. As a matter of fact, after the cross match is set on fire, it soon burns the wood away, and the pressure of the two side matches will cause it to spring out so that neither catches fire.

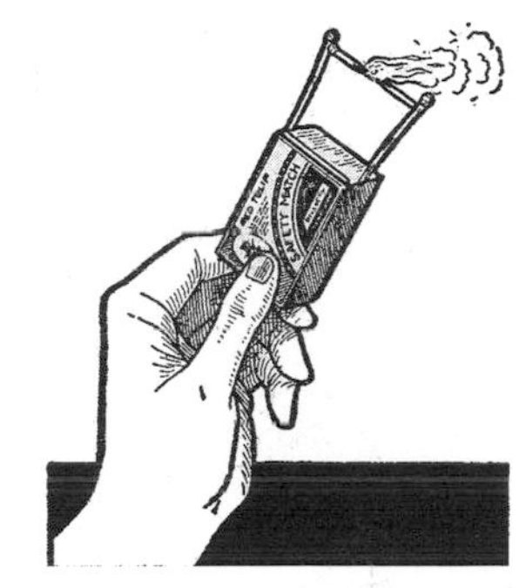

Which matches will burn?

— The Broken-Match Trick —

The effect of this very pretty and effective table trick is as follows: The performer breaks off six small pieces of wooden match ½ in. or less in length. Showing his hands to be empty, he places five of these, one at a time, into his left hand. He then takes the sixth piece of match and places it in his pocket. But when he opens his left hand, the sixth piece is found to have joined the others in his left hand! This may be repeated several times. Finally, the performer, in order to show that he himself does not place an extra piece of match in his hand, requests some onlooker to put them there himself. In spite of the fact that his hands are examined and the pieces of match are placed in the hand by some onlooker, they nevertheless continue to multiply. Apparently nothing can prevent the five pieces of match from increasing to six!

As the initiated reader will have guessed, the trick consists of adding an extra, seventh piece to those placed in the left hand. This extra piece is palmed between the second and third fingers of the right hand, thus leaving the forefinger free. The pieces of match are picked up, one at a time, by the thumb and forefinger of the right hand, then placed in the left hand. For the first four times, this act is free from trickery. But on the fifth occasion, as the fifth piece is added, the concealed piece is also dropped into the left hand. That hand is then quickly closed, thereby concealing the extra piece. The right hand is now shown to be empty, and the sixth piece is picked up and seemingly placed in the pocket. In fact, it is still retained between the fingers and immediately withdrawn from the pocket, ready for the next trial. On the left hand being opened, the six pieces of match are, of course, shown.

In placing the matches in the left hand, it is often possible to throw them quite a distance through the air. The two pieces may also be thus thrown without detection, on the fifth occasion. This greatly adds to the effectiveness of the trick.

It now remains to explain how the matches multiply when the onlooker himself places the matches in the magician's hand. In this case, the performer's left hand is first carefully examined, and the attention of the onlookers is also called to the fact that there is nothing on the table. The left hand is held out, and the sitter is invited to place the matches in it himself. While indicating this hand to the sitter, the magician points to the palm of his left hand with the forefinger of his right hand, as though showing him where to place the pieces. This naturally brings the second and third fingers of the right hand beneath the left hand, and the concealed piece of match is dropped onto the table. The back of the left hand is now quickly lowered onto this piece, thus concealing it, while the counting continues. The sixth piece is placed in the pocket, as before, and the performer rapidly turns over his opened hand, thus turning the five pieces of match in his hand onto the sixth piece on the table. The illusion is perfect, and six pieces of match are disclosed.

Among other methods of concealing the piece of match are the following: between the fingers; in the crease formed by the base of the thumb (the back of the hand); and between the fingertip and the underside of the table, when the hand is so held that the tip of the finger falls just below the table. The resourceful performer will vary the trick more or less every time he does it, thus rendering its discovery almost impossible.

— A Perfect Match —

The performer exhibits six matches. Three have red tips and three have blue tips. The matches are examined. No distinguishing marks are found beyond the colored tips. The matches go behind the performer's back, and he correctly calls the color of the tip before bringing each match forward.

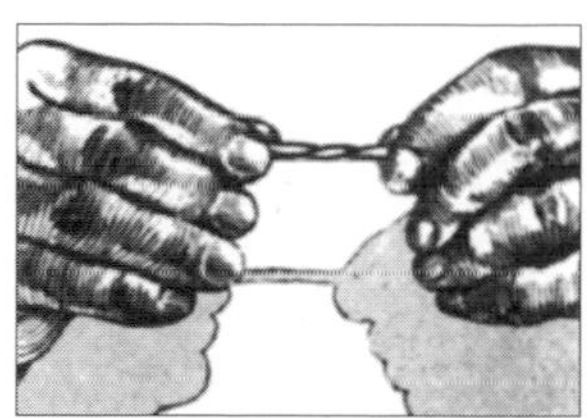

Preparing the Match

Telling which match is which is simple if you have previously twisted the blue-tipped matches lightly between your fingers, as shown in the illustration—not hard, just a gentle turn to strain the wood fibers. The match will immediately spring back into shape, but by turning the match head behind your back, you can easily spot the prepared matches.

— Torn and Restored Cigarette Paper —

The magician borrows an ordinary cigarette paper. Taking it with the tips of his fingers, he tears it across and across again, until it has been torn into eight small pieces. Then, rolling these pieces together, he produces the paper whole again, as before. As the reader has already suspected, the secret consists of substituting a whole piece of cigarette paper for the torn pieces. The value of the trick is in concealing this whole piece, then afterward substituting it for the torn pieces.

A very excellent method of doing so is as follows: The whole piece of paper, folded into a small ball, is held between the first and second fingers, near the tips. Now, taking the second piece of paper with the fingers of the left hand, the performer transfers it to the fingers of the right hand, which effectually conceals the ball of paper beneath it. Both sides of the right hand and the left hand may now be shown to be empty. The paper is then torn, and torn again, each time showing that the left hand is empty. The small pieces of paper conceal the duplicate ball beneath them.

The pieces of paper are now rolled into a ball; in the act of doing this, the second finger of the right hand is pushed slightly forward, so that the duplicate paper will be pushed under and into close contact with the torn strips, forming what appears to be one ball with them. At this point, both hands may be shown to be empty. The ball of paper is then further rolled. While doing so, the duplicate ball is rolled to the top of the pile and the torn strips are rolled into the place of the original duplicate ball—that is, between the first and second fingers of the right hand. The performer now unrolls the duplicate paper, which conceals the original torn strips, and exhibits it. When properly done, this is a capital and very effective little trick.

— Smoky Mind Reading —

Here's a mind-reading trick with cigarettes. A new pack is broken open. The performer turns his back and asks a spectator to push a pin into any cigarette, saying, "Better turn it over so that I can't possibly see it." Of course, you are way out in front for the rest of the stunt, lifting the cigarettes one at a time to the forehead until you come to the right one. The method is simple: All cigarettes are packed with the trademark facing one way, usually toward the top of the pack. Turning the selected cigarette over, supposedly to conceal the pin, actually tells you which one to pick.

— Matchstick Magic —

Figure 1 Figure 2 Figure 3

A couple of match tricks: The first one involves causing a match to stand unsupported on a piece of wood. Lean the match against a cup, head down on a piece of scrap wood, as shown in *Figure 1.* Ignite the head, then quickly blow out the flame. The head will "fuse" to the board sufficiently to hold it in place, as in *Figure 2.* In the second trick (*Figure 3*), you split a match in half and ask someone to drop it in such a way that it will remain on edge. Of course, there's only one way to do it, and that involves breaking the match at the center to form a V shape.

— The Disappearing Matches —

The following little trick, which is both pretty and effective, is to cause the disappearance of five or six matches, one at a time, from the fingertips. To perform it successfully, the conjurer must wear a ring that is a trifle too large for him, on the third finger of the right hand. Holding a match between his forefinger and thumb, and tossing his hand to cover the action, the performer must slip it under the ring on the back of the hand.

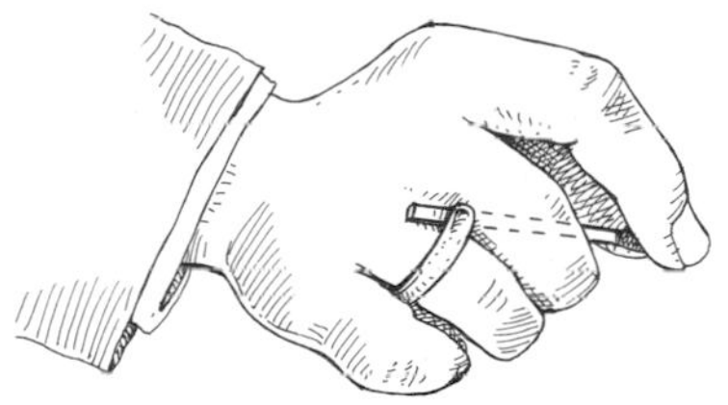

Concealing a match in the oversized ring

The movement is more fully shown in the accompanying illustration.

The other matches may be vanished in the same manner, then recovered again by a reverse action to that explained above. The fingers should be spread apart, to make it a really mystifying impromptu trick.

— The Floating Cigarette —

The secret of a bewitched cigarette is shown in the illustration. A length of black thread with a pin at one end is wound around the magician's coat button, and a pin is stuck on the inside of the coat until the performer is ready to execute the trick. When no one is looking, the pin is pushed into the end of the cigarette, which is then dropped into the bottle. The bottle is moved forward until the thread supports the cigarette; then, moving the bottle back and forth causes the cigarette to rise and fall. This trick should be performed only under dim lights. When the cigarette and bottle are handed around the table, the pin is discreetly pulled out to drop in your lap.

— Tying a Cigarette —

Can you tie a cigarette into a knot, then untie it, without breaking the paper? Sounds impossible? Just remove a square piece of unwrinkled cellophane from a cigarette package and wrap it around the cigarette, leaving a 1 in. margin at either end. Twist the ends tightly, then knot the cigarette. When it is straightened out and the cellophane removed, the cigarette will be unbroken.

— Match Mates —

The series of photos shows an easy match trick. Two matches are lit, then one is held aside in a vertical position while the other, in a horizontal position, is blown out. The unlit end of the burning match is touched to the head of the smoking match, and the horizontal match relights.

Blowing out the horizontal match

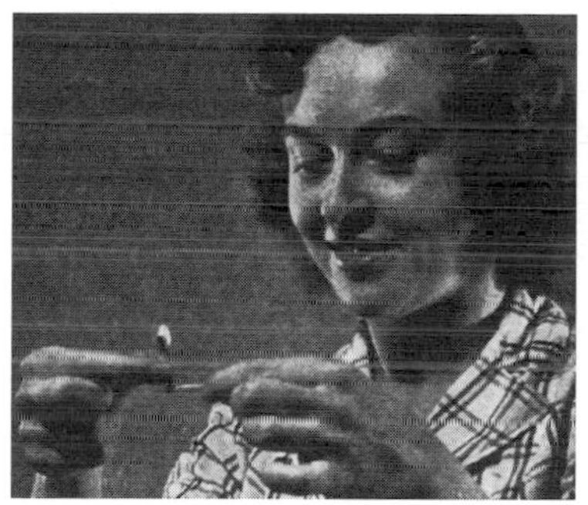

Touching the unlit match head to the opposite end of the lit match

The unlit match ignites!

{CHAPTER 4}

THE ART *of* MISDIRECTION

Eye Don't Know

— The Magic Candle and Flag —

This is a trick that can easily be performed by the amateur with very mystifying effect, and the necessary apparatus is simple to make. The trick is this: A candlestick, with a candle in it, is placed on a table. A cylinder is shown to be empty, after which it is placed over the candle so that the latter is concealed. The magician makes a few appropriate passes, at the same time saying one of the seven magic words, of which "abracadabra" is the most potent. When the cylinder is removed, the candle has disappeared and the tube is shown to be empty. Then a flag or handkerchief is extracted from it. While the audience is still wondering how this was done, the operator reaches into a coat pocket, produces the lit candle, and places it back in the candlestick.

The apparatus required consists of the trick candlestick as illustrated,

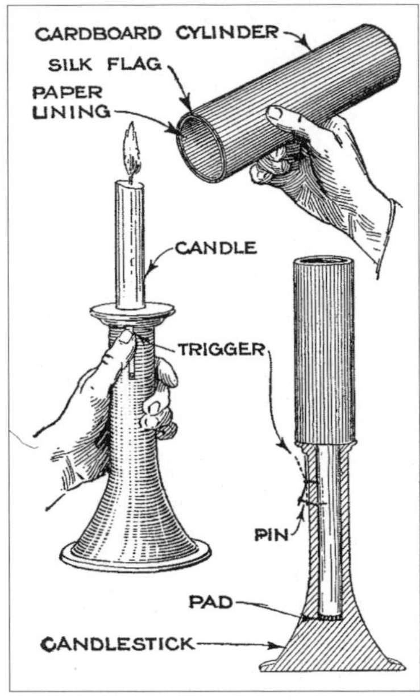

two imitation candles, a cardboard cylinder, and a silk flag or handkerchief. The base of the candlestick is hollow. When the cylinder is placed over it, a trigger is pressed that allows the candle to drop out of sight into the hollow base. The flag is folded and placed like a lining within the cylinder, kept out of sight of the audience by a paper lining, as indicated in the drawing. The cylinder is prepared and the second candle placed in the magician's pocket before the performance. This candle has a match head for a wick; as the candle is taken from the pocket, the match is struck on a piece of sandpaper that is pinned in a convenient place on the inside of the coat.

The candlestick can be bought ready-made, or it may be made from wood. The hole in which the candle drops must be large enough to make a snug but free fit, and deep enough to conceal the candle entirely when it is resting on the bottom. A small wire pin projects through the candlestick just far enough to hold the candle in place, yet very little movement will release it. A bent strip of sheet metal serves as a trigger, and this is fastened at its center to the candlestick, very loosely. When the cylinder is placed over the candle, the performer presses the trigger and lets the candle fall. In this position, the top of the candle should be even with the wire pin, so that when the second lit candle is set in the candlestick, it will rest on top of the first one.

The candles can be made from metal, paper tubes, or wood. If tubes are used, corks are inserted into the ends to hold the wicks. In any case, have a wick on one candle and a small hole for a wick on the other. Enamel them white. For the light effect in the second candle, a match end is inserted in the wick hole. The cylinder that is put over the candle to hide it can be made from cardboard or sheet metal and finished as desired. Fold the flag and place it so as to be close to one end of the tube. When taking the flag from the cylinder, hold the cylinder and the paper lining tightly together, at the end farthest from the flag, so that the latter can be pulled out without disturbing the paper.

— An Electric Illusion Box —

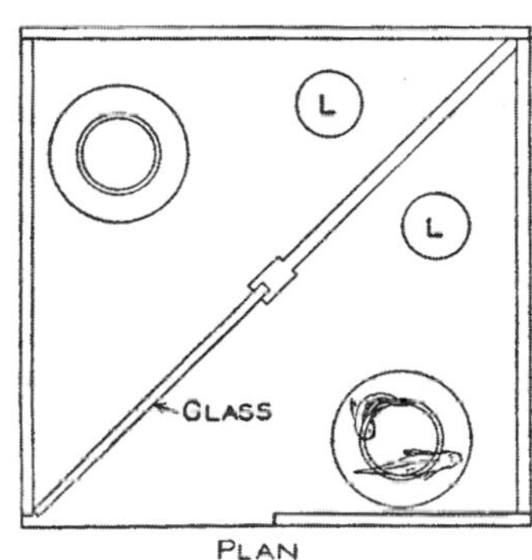

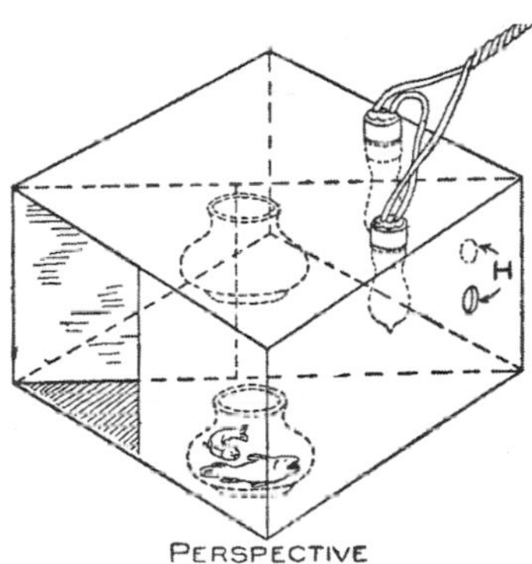

Construction of magic boxes

The accompanying engravings show a most interesting form of electrically operated illusion, consisting of a box divided diagonally and each division alternately lit with an electric lamp. By means of an automatic thermostat arranged in the electric circuit, causing the lamps to light successively, an aquarium apparently without fish one moment is swarming with live goldfish in the next instant, an empty vase viewed through the opening in the box is suddenly filled with flowers, or an empty cigar box is seen and immediately filled with cigars.

The electric magic boxes shown are made of metal and finished with oxidized copper. But for ordinary use they can be made of wood in the same shape and size. The magic boxes are about 12 in. square and

8½ in. high for parlor use, and are 18 in. square and 10½ in. high for use in window displays. There is a partition arranged diagonally in the box, as shown in the plan view, which completely divides the box into two parts. Half the partition is fitted with a plain, clear glass, as shown. The partition and interior of the box are rendered non-reflecting by painting them matte black. When it is made of wood, a door must be provided on the side or rear to make changes of exhibits. If the box is made large enough, or in the larger size mentioned, openings may be made in the bottom for this purpose. The openings can also be used to perform the magic trick of allowing two people to place their heads in the box and change from one to the other.

The electric globes are inserted, as shown at *LL*, through the top of the box, one in each division. When the rear part is illuminated, any article arranged within that part will be visible to the spectator looking into the box through the front opening; however, when the front part is illuminated and the back left dark, any article placed therein will be reflected in the glass, which takes the same position to the observer as the one in the rear. Thus, a plain aquarium is set in the rear part and one with swimming fish placed in the front, and with the proper illumination one is changed, as it appears, into the other. When using this as a window display, place the goods in one part and the price in the other. Many other changes can be made at the will of the operator.

Electric lamps may be controlled by various means to produce different effects. Lamps may be connected in parallel and each turned on or off by means of a hand-operated switch or the button on the lamp socket. Or, if desired, a hand-operated adjustable resistance may be included in the circuit of each lamp for causing the object to fade away gradually or reappear slowly.

Instead of changing the current by hand, this may be done automatically by connecting the lamps in parallel on the lighting circuit, with each connected in series with a thermostatic switch plug provided with a heating coil that operates to open and close the circuit through the respective lamp.

When no electric current is available, matches or candles may be used and inserted through the holes, *H*, as shown in the sketch.

— A One-Piece Bracelet Cut from a Calling Card —

A trick that will amuse and interest both old and young can be performed with a calling card, cigarette paper, or other similar material. The material is cut with a scissors or knife, as indicated in the diagram. The card is shown, and the performer announces that he will pass his hand through the card, making a bracelet of it. He will, of course, be challenged. He proceeds as follows: He folds the card lengthwise and cuts through two thicknesses from 1 to 2, 3 to 4, and so on; then he opens the card and cuts from 1 to 13. By stretching the paper, as shown in the sketch, he can readily pass his hand through the card. The spectators are soon trying to duplicate the trick.

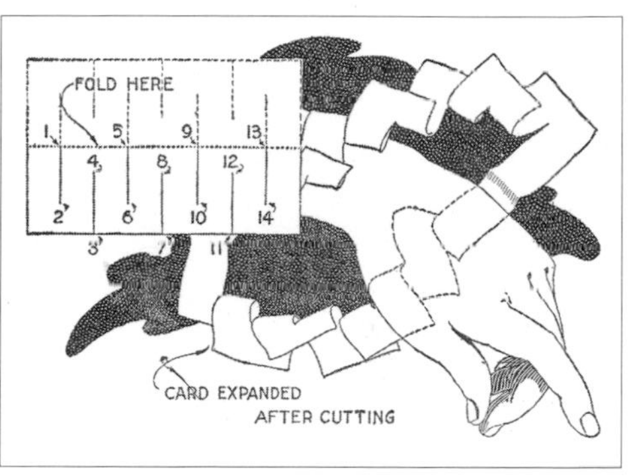

It is hard to imitate a quick and skillful performance of this simple trick.

— A Trunk Mystery —

Doubtless every person has seen the trunk mystery, the effect of which is as follows: A trunk mounted on four legs is brought out on the stage and proven to be empty by turning it all the way around, to show that there is nothing on the back. Pieces of plate glass are placed along the back, sides, and front, the trunk is closed and given a swift turn, and then it is opened. To the amazement of all, a lady steps out, appearing to have come from nowhere. The secret of this trick is very simple, and the trunk can be made up very cheaply.

In the back of the trunk is a movable panel with a shelf exactly the

A SHELF AND PANEL ARE SET AT RIGHT ANGLES TO FORM A PLACE AT THE BACK FOR THE ASSISTANT TO CONCEAL HERSELF, NO MATTER WHICH WAY THE TRUNK IS TURNED TO FACE THE AUDIENCE.

same size as the panel attached to its bottom, forming a right angle and jutting outward from the back and bottom of the trunk. The corner of the right angle is hinged to the bottom of the trunk. The back panel can be turned in until it rests on the bottom of the trunk; when this is done, the shelf part rises and takes its place, making the back of the trunk appear solid.

When the trunk is brought out onstage, the assistant is crouching on the shelf, behind and outside the trunk. The trunk can then be shown to be empty. This is all very simple until the trunk is turned around, when it takes skill not to give the trick away. As soon as the performer starts to turn the trunk around, the assistant shifts her weight on the panel, thus causing it to fall inward and bringing the shelf up to make the back appear solid. The assistant is now inside the trunk, and the back can be shown to be clear of any apparatus. When the trunk is turned to the front again, the lady repeats the previous operation in the opposite direction, thus bringing her body to the back of the trunk again.

To make the trick appear more difficult, glass plates are made to insert in the ends, front, and back of the trunk. In making the trunk, the back should be the same size as the bottom. Fit the piece of glass for the back into a light frame, similar to a window frame. This frame is hinged to the bottom of the trunk and is ½ in. smaller all around than the back of the trunk. This is so that the two pieces of glass can be put in the ends, and it also allows the back frame and glass to fall flush in the bottom of the trunk. A few rubber bumpers are fastened in the bottom of the trunk to ensure that the glass falls without noise. The best way to work this is for the performer to let the frame down with his right hand while he is closing up the front with his left.

As soon as the trunk is closed, the assistant again shifts her weight to cause the movable panel to fall in. The trunk can be turned to show the back or whirled around and turned to the front again, then opened up, whereupon the assistant steps out, bows to the audience, and leaves the stage.

— A Mystic Fortune-Teller —

Fortune-telling by means of weights striking glasses or bottles is quite mysterious if controlled in a manner that cannot be seen by the audience. The performer can propose two strikes for "no" and three for "yes" to answer questions. Any kind of bottles, glass, or cups may be used. In the bottles, the pendulum can be suspended from the cork, and in the glasses from small tripods set on the table.

The secret of the trick is as follows: A rubber tube with a bulb attached to each end is placed under a rug, one bulb being located under one table leg and the other near the chair of the performer. This is set at some distance from the table, where it can be pressed with the foot. Someone selects a pendulum. The performer gazes intently at it and presses the bulb under his foot, lightly at first. Then, by watching the

THE ROCKING OF THE TABLE IS CAUSED BY THE PRESSURE OF AIR IN THE BULB UNDER THE FOOT, THE MOVEMENT CAUSING THE PENDULUM TO SWING AND STRIKE THE GLASS.

swaying of the pendulum selected, he will know when to give the second impulse, and he continues until the weight strikes the glass. As the pendulums are of different lengths, they must necessarily swing at different rates per second. The impulses must be given at the proper time, or else the pendulum will be retarded instead of increased in amplitude. A table with four legs is best, and the leg diagonally opposite the one with the bulb beneath it must not touch the carpet or floor. This can be arranged by placing pieces of cardboard under the other two legs.

— Rubber-Band-Change Trick —

The trick of changing a rubber band from the first and second fingers to the third and fourth, if done quickly, can be performed without detection by the audience. The band on the first two fingers is shown to the spectator, as in *Figure 1,* with the back of the hand up. The hand is then turned over and the rubber band drawn out quickly, as shown in *Figure 2,* in such a manner as to give the impression that the band is whole and on the two fingers. While doing this, quickly fold all the fingers so that their ends enter the band, then turn the hand over and let go of the band. Then show the back with the fingers doubled up. In reality, the fingers will be in the band, as in *Figure 3,* and the back will still show the band on the first two fingers. Quickly straighten out all the fingers, and the band will snap over the last two fingers, as in *Figure 4.*

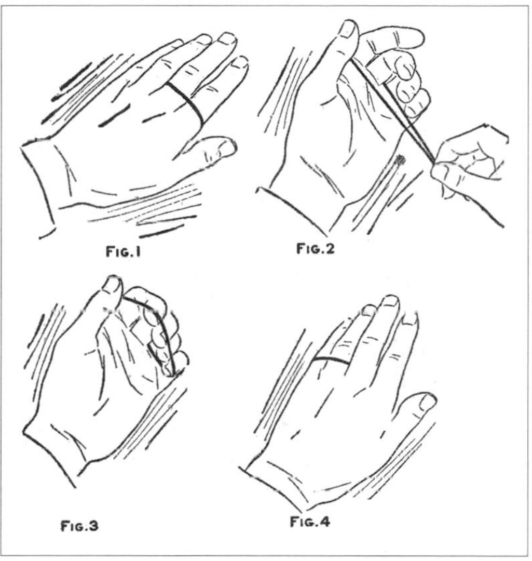

TRANSFERRING THE RUBBER BAND FROM THE FIRST TWO FINGERS TO THE LAST PAIR, LIKE MAGIC

— MAGIC CANDLES EXPLAINED —

Clever and baffling though it may be, the "Magic-Candle Trick" may be performed easily and with professional skill by a person who has made a few simple preparations. The illustration shows the candles arranged on a table made of a music stand.

Candles, cigars, or pencils may be used, but for the purpose of this description, the former will be used. The candles are of different colors but the same size and weight.

The manipulation proceeds as follows: Exhibit a tube of brass, cardboard, or other suitable material, just large enough to contain a candle. Then retire from the room, leaving the tube on the table while a spectator selects one of the candles and places it into the tube, covering the end of the latter securely with a small cap. The other candles are hidden before the performer is permitted to return. The trick is to announce the color of the candle contained in the box by merely passing the hand over it several times. The box and the candle are passed around for inspection and will bear it if properly prepared.

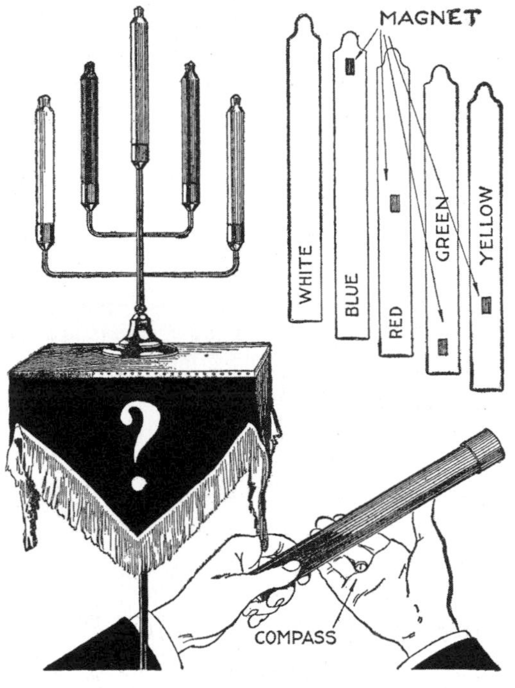

MYSTERIOUS PASSES OVER THE CONCEALED CANDLE ARE MADE, AND ITS COLOR IS THEN ANNOUNCED.

The secret of the trick is this: The first candle—for example, the white one—is unprepared. The second, a blue one, has concealed in it, ½ in. from the top, a small piece of magnetized steel. The third candle, a red one, has a similar bar concealed at the middle. The fourth candle has a magnetized bar ½ in. from the bottom, and the fifth has the bar at a point halfway between the middle and the bottom. The candles are made of two pieces of wood, glued together like a pencil, and the magnets may readily be embedded in them.

The performer hides a small compass in his palm. It is held in place by a wire clip, gripped between the second and third fingers near the knuckles. A wave of the hand over the tube containing a candle will affect the compass if any candle other than the white one is used. Its needle will vibrate when approaching the concealed magnet, and by quickly determining the position of the magnet, the performer can announce the color. Those who offer guesses usually insist that some electric device is being used.

— Fireside Dissolving Views —

To those interested in amateur theatricals, the following method of showing dissolving views in the firelight of pipe dreams and mind pictures will be appreciated.

A frame made of light material, *A* (*Figure 1*), covered with red cloth and chalked to represent brick, is placed at the center of the stage. The central opening, representing the fireplace, must be rather large, about 12 ft. wide and 7 ft. high, because it is at the back of this opening that the pictures are produced. From the chimney back, 2½ ft. behind this opening, the sides, *B*, of the fireplace slope outward to the imitation brick-work. The walls of the fireplace are

THE TABLEAU IS PLAYED OUT BEHIND THE SCREENS, AND IT IS DIMLY SEEN THROUGH THE FIREPLACE OPENING WHEN THE LIGHTS ARE PROPERLY CONTROLLED AND THE SCREENS ARE DRAWN ASIDE SLOWLY.

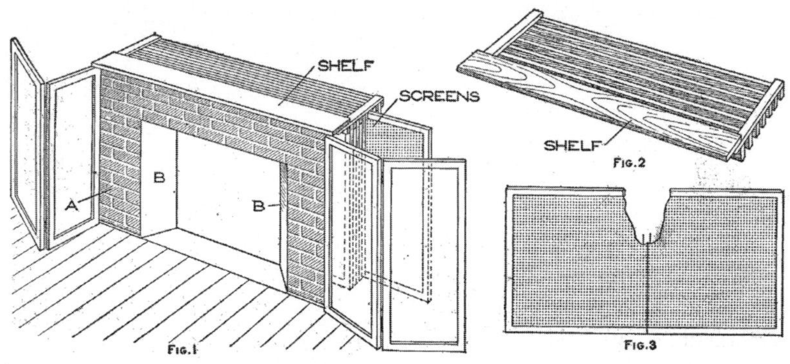

Frames made of light material and covered with black mosquito netting serve as screens that are operated in runs located behind the fireplace. The fireplace is made up in a like manner and penciled to represent brick.

covered with fireproof material, for safety, and painted black. Then ashes are rubbed on the chimney back and scattered over the hearthstone, to make the appearance more realistic.

The chimney back is removable. In fact, it is one of a series of a half-dozen screens, the others being behind it. The proper manipulation of these screens, together with changing lights, gives the audience the illusion of dissolving views of the dreams that are being acted out directly behind the screens.

The screens are carried in a light frame, the top of which is shown in *Figure 2,* with runs. The runs are made of narrow strips of wood fastened to the underside of two end pieces, into which the screen frames slide. Corresponding strips are placed in a suitable position on the floor, to keep the screens steady while sliding. The frames holding the run pieces are longer than the chimney back is wide, and the upper one is placed as high as the brickwork, the shelf, or the mantel over the fireplace. It is an extension of the upper part, or frame.

The screens are in pairs, as shown in *Figure 3.* Each one extends to the center of the fireplace. They consist of light frames covered with black mosquito netting. The upper and lower sides of the frame are sand-papered smooth, so that they will move easily in the runs. The vertical sides of a pair of screen frames that meet in the center of the fireplace are made of one strand of wire instead of wood, so that their motion will not be noticeable. To complete the apparatus, andirons and a gas log are needed in the fireplace, as well as whatever arrangements are necessary for the action of the views to be shown behind the screens.

If gas is available, a fake log is used in the fireplace and connected by pipe to the gas footlights. Four or five jets are located on the floor just in back of the screens. A narrow board, painted black, is placed in front of the lights, which should be wide enough to conceal the lights from the spectators and reflect the light on each tableau. If the light is thrown above the imitation brickwork, then it should be made higher.

In most halls, electric lights are used instead of gas. In this case, ordinary logs are piled in the fireplace on the andirons, and one or more red globes are introduced to produce the effect of glowing embers. Gas is more effective, however, because it is not easy to get a gradual rise and fall in the glow of electric lights. Four or five footlights are sufficient.

The gas log is turned low to make the stage dimly lit, and the tableau to be shown is all arranged behind the chimney back and the screens. There should be barely sufficient light to reveal a bachelor on the hearthstone, smoking in the gloaming. Then the chimney back parts almost imperceptibly; that is, the screens of the first pair are gradually pulled apart. The footlights and gas log are gradually turned on, and the tableau behind the fireplace, being more brightly illuminated, is dimly seen through the series of screens.

Slowly, the successive pairs of screens are drawn aside, and the tableau becomes quite distinct. Then the process is reversed, the screens are gradually replaced, the lights are lowered, and the dream fades away, brightens and fades again, brightens and fades, until gone entirely. The screens are always slowly moving while the tableau is exposed, and this achieves the illusory effect. It is evident that the success of this plan depends principally on the coordination with which the screens are operated. "Cinderella," and many other tales based on the vagaries of the mind and having their source in glowing embers, can thus be presented.

— A Miniature "Pepper's Ghost" Illusion —

Probably many readers have seen a "Pepper's Ghost" illusion at some amusement place. As shown here, the audience is generally seated in a dark room, at the end of which is a stage with black hangings. A member of the audience is invited onto the stage, where he is placed in an upright open coffin. A white shroud is thrown over this body. His clothes and flesh gradually fade away until nothing but his skeleton remains, which immediately begins to dance a horrible rattling jig. The skeleton then fades away, and the man is restored again.

A simple explanation is given in the *Model Engineer.* Between the audience and the coffin is a sheet of transparent glass, inclined at an angle so as to reflect objects located behind the scenes, but so clear as to be invisible to the audience and the man in the coffin. At the beginning, the stage is lit only from behind the glass. Hence, the coffin and its occupant are seen through the glass very plainly. The lights in front of the glass (behind the scenes) are now raised very gradually as those behind the glass are turned down, until it is dark there. The perfectly black surface behind the glass now acts like the silver backing for a mirror, and the object on which the light is now turned—in this case, the skeleton—is reflected in the glass, appearing to the audience as if really occupying the space.

The model, which requires no special skill except that of carpentry, is constructed as shown in the drawings.

The box containing the stage should be 14 by 7 by 7½ in. (interior dimensions). The box need not be made of particularly good wood, because the entire interior, with the exception of the glass, figures, and lights, should be colored a dull black. This can be done by painting with a solution of lampblack in turpentine. If everything is not black, especially the joints and background near the figure, *A,* the illusion will be spoiled.

The glass should be the clearest possible and must be thoroughly cleansed. Its edges should nowhere be visible, and it should be free from scratches and imperfections. The figure, *A,* should be a doll about four inches high, dressed in brilliant,

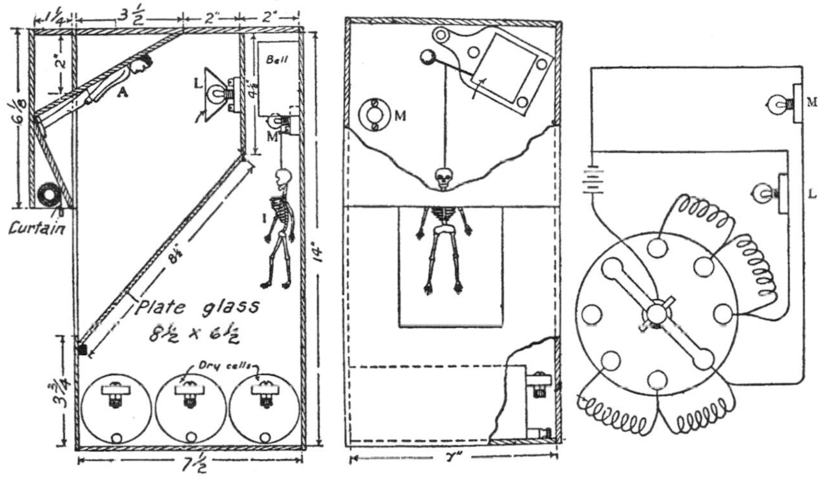

CONSTRUCTION OF THE "PEPPER'S GHOST" ILLUSION

light-colored garments. The skeleton is made of papier-mâché and can be bought at Japanese stores. It should preferably be one with arms suspended by small spiral springs, giving it a limp, loose-jointed effect. The method of causing the skeleton to dance is shown in the front view. The figure is hung from the neck by a blackened stiff wire attached to the hammer wire of an electric bell, from which the gong has been removed. When the bell works, he will kick against the rear wall and wave his arms up and down, thus giving as realistic a dance as anyone could expect from a skeleton.

The lights, *L* and *M*, should be miniature electric lamps. These can be run by three dry cells. They need to give a fairly strong light, especially *L*, which should have a conical tin reflector to increase its brilliancy and prevent it from being reflected in the glass.

Because the stage should be some distance from the audience to aid the illusion, both the angle of the glass and the inclination of the doll, *A*, have been so designed that if the stage is placed on a mantel or other high shelf, the image of *A* will appear upright to an observer sitting in a chair some distance away.

If it is desired to place the box lower down, other angles for the image and glass may be found necessary; the proper tilt can be found readily by experiment.

The electric connections are so simple that they are not shown in the drawings. All that is necessary is a two-point switch, by which either *L* or *M* can be placed in circuit with the battery, as well as a press button in circuit with the bell and its cell.

For a gradual transformation, a double-pointed rheostat could be used: as one light dims, the other increases in brilliancy, by the insertion and removal of resistance coils.

With a clear glass and a dark room, this model has proved to be fully as bewildering as its prototype.

— The Bent Watch —

Borrow a watch and remark that "it is really a very peculiar watch—it appears to be quite soft," or something to that effect. Then take the watch between your fingers and apparently bend it backward and forward, as though it were a piece of tin!

The secret lies in an optical illusion. Take the watch between the fingers, each hand on the back and both thumbs on the front, or face, then hold the watch with the dial toward yourself, as shown in the illustration.

Now bend your hands outward, at the same time bringing your fingers closer together and the watch nearer to you. Reverse the motion by pushing the watch from you, at the same time bringing the wrists closer together and the fingers farther apart. The result, if you alternate these motions quickly, will be that the watch will appear to be bent almost double with each motion of the hands.

This is hardly a trick all by itself, but it may be introduced as a sort of byplay to any trick in which a watch has to be borrowed.

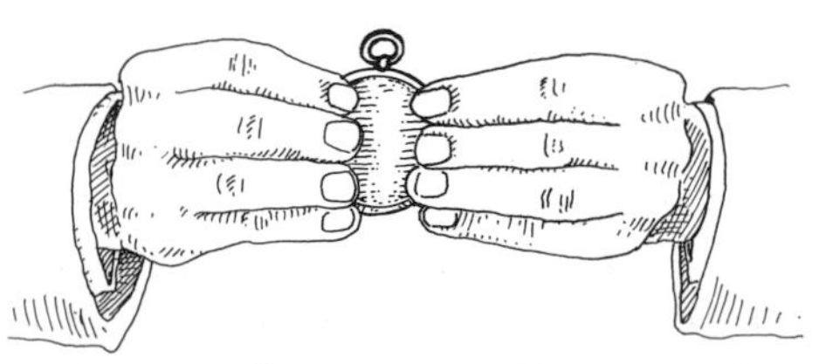

The soft watch

— Balloon-Ascension Illusion —

In these days of startling revelations in aircraft flight, we are prepared to see any day now some marvelous machine-driven bird cutting figure eights all over the sky above our heads. One boy recently took advantage of this state of expectancy to have an evening's harmless amusement, through an illusion that deceived even the most incredulous. He caused a whole hotel full of people to gaze open-mouthed at a sort of "Zeppelin XXIII," which skimmed along the distant horizon, just visible against the dark evening sky, disappearing only to reappear again, and working the whole crowd up to a frenzy of excitement. And all he used was a black thread, a big piece of cardboard, and a pair of field glasses.

He stretched the thread between two buildings about 100 ft. apart, in an endless belt passing through a screw eye at either end. On this thread he fastened a cardboard cutout of a dirigible—not much to look at in daytime, but most deceptive at dusk. By pulling one or the other string, he moved the "airship" in either direction. He took the precaution of stretching his thread just beyond the a hedge and thus kept overly inquisitive people at a safe distance. He also saw to it that there was a black background at either end, so that the reversing of the direction of the craft would not be noticed.

To attract the crowd, he had a confederate stand looking at the moving ship through field glasses, which at once gave the suggestion of distance and materially heightened the illusion. When the interest of the crowd was at its height, the "aeronaut" pulled his craft out of sight and let the disillusion come when the light of day laid bare his fraud.

— The Invisible Light —

The magician places two common wax candles on a table, one of them burning brightly, the other without a light. Members of the audience are allowed to inspect both the table and the candles. The magician walks over to the burning candle and shades the light for a few seconds. He turns to the audience with his hands a few inches apart, showing that there is nothing between them. At the same time, he says that he has a light between his hands, invisible to the audience, with which he is going to light the other candle. He then walks over to the other candle and, in plain sight of the audience, lights the candle apparently with nothing.

In reality, the magician has a very fine wire in his hand that he is heating while he stands over the lit candle, as the audience gazes on but sees nothing. He turns to the other candle and touches the heated wire to a grain of phosphorus that has been previously concealed in the wick, thus causing it to light.

Watch *the* Hand

— A Skidoo-Skidee Trick —

In a recent issue of *Popular Mechanics,* an article on "the Turning Card Puzzle" was described and illustrated. Here is a much better trick. About the time when the expression "skidoo" first began to be used, the following trick, called "Skidoo and Skidee," was invented, and it created much merriment. Unless the trick is thoroughly understood, for some it will turn one way, for others the opposite way, while for still others it will not revolve at all. One person became red in the face shouting "Skidoo" and "Skidee" at it, but the thing would not move at all! He finally threw the trick into the fire, and a new one had to be made. Very few people are able to make it turn both ways at will, and therein lies the trick.

Take a piece of hardwood ⅜ in. square and about 9 in. long. In one of the edges, cut a series of notches, as indicated in *Figure 1.* Then slightly taper the end marked *B* until it is nicely rounded, as shown in *Figure 2.* Next, make an arm of a two-arm windmill, such as boys make. Make a hole through the center of this one arm. Enlarge the hole slightly, enough to allow a common pin to hold the arm to the end, *B,* but not to interfere with the revolving arm. Two or three of these arms may have to be made before one is secured that is of the exact proportions to catch the vibrations right.

To operate the trick, grip the stick

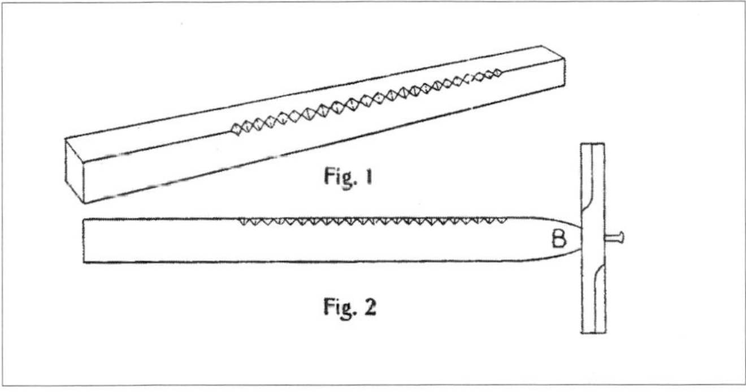

How to cut the notches

firmly in one hand, and with the forward and backward motion of the other hand, allow the first finger to slide along the top edge and the second finger along the side; the thumbnail will then vibrate along the notches, thus making the arm revolve in one direction. To make the arm revolve in the opposite direction—keeping the hand moving all the time, so the observer will not detect the change that it makes—allow the forefinger to slide along the top, as in the other movement, but with the thumb and second finger changing places. For example, in the first movement you scratch the notches with the nail of the second finger when the hand is coming toward the body, thus producing two different vibrations.

In order to make it work perfectly, you must of course say, "Skidoo," when you begin the first movement, and then, no matter how fast the little arm is revolving when changed to the second movement, you must say, "Skidee," and then the arm will immediately stop and begin revolving in the opposite direction. When you use the magic words, the little arm will obey your commands instantly, and your audience will be mystified. If any members of your audience presume to dispute you, or think that they can do the same, let them try it. You will no doubt be accused of blowing or drawing in your breath, or many other things, to make the arm operate. At least it is amusing. Try it and see.

— String-and-Ball Trick —

Stopping a ball on a string at a desired point is a technique understood by almost every person, but to make one that can be worked only when the operator so desires is a mysterious trick. Procure a wooden ball, about 2 in. in diameter, and cut it into two equal parts. Insert a small peg in the flat surface of one half, a little to one side of the center, as shown in the illustration, and allow the end to project about 3/16 in. The flat surface of the other half is cut out concave, as shown, to make it ½ in. deep. The two halves are then glued together, and a hole is drilled centrally on the division line for a string to pass through it.

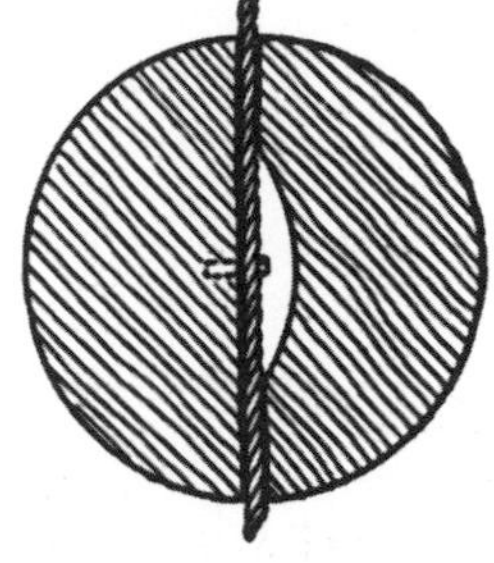

THE GLUED BALL HALVES WITH A STRING PASSING THROUGH

THE PEG ALLOWS YOU TO STOP THE BALL AT WILL

To do the trick, hold an end of the string in each hand tightly and draw it taut with the ball at the top, then slacken the string enough to allow the ball to slide down the string. To stop the ball at any point, pull the string taut.

Before handing out the ball and string for inspection by the audience, push the string from each side of the ball and turn it slightly to throw it off the peg. This will allow the string to pass freely through the ball, and then the ball cannot be stopped at will. To replace the string, reverse the operation.

— Magic Spirit Hand —

This magic hand is made of wax and given to the audience for examination, along with a board that is suspended by four pieces of common picture-frame wire. The hand is placed on the board and answers, by rapping, any question asked by members of the audience. The hand and the board may be examined at any time, yet the rapping can be continued, though both are surrounded by the audience.

The secret of this spirit hand is as follows: The hand is prepared by concealing in the wrist a few soft iron plates, the wrist being afterward bound with black velvet as shown in *Figure 1.* The board is hollow, the top being made of thin veneer (*Figure 2*). A small magnet, *A,* is connected to a small, flat pocket-lamp battery, *B.* The board is suspended by four lengths of picture-frame wire, one of which, *E,* is connected to the battery and another, *D,* to the magnet. The other wires, *F* and *G,* are only holding wires. All the wires are fastened to a small ornamental switch, *H,* which is fitted with a connecting plug at

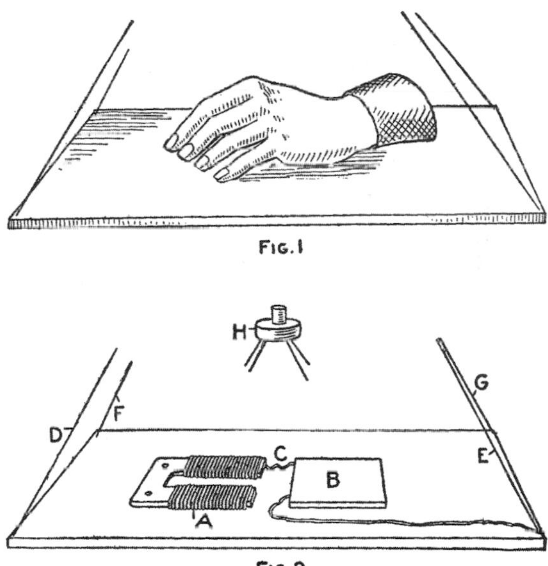

THE WAX HAND ON THE BOARD AND THE ELECTRIC CONNECTIONS THAT HELP IT MOVE

the top. The plug can be taken out or put in as desired.

The top of the board must be made to open or slide off, so that when the battery is exhausted, a new one can be installed. Everything must be firmly fixed to the board and the hollow space filled in with wax, which will make the board sound solid when tapped.

In presenting the trick, the performer shows the hand and board with wires and switch for examination, while keeping the plug concealed in his right hand. When receiving the board back, he secretly pushes the plug into the switch, which is held in the right hand. The hand is then placed on the board over the magnet. When the performer wishes the hand to move, he pushes the plug in. This turns on the current and causes the magnet to attract the iron in the wrist, which will therefore make the hand rap. The switch can be made similar to an ordinary push button, so that the rapping may be easily controlled without detection by the audience.

— The Floating Knife —

Another trick, which is simply an illusion, is shown in the photo. It looks as if the knife is glued to the palm of the hand, but the guests don't see the index finger of the right hand, which holds the knife. To all appearances, the right hand is grasping the left wrist, and one doesn't pause to count the number of fingers visible.

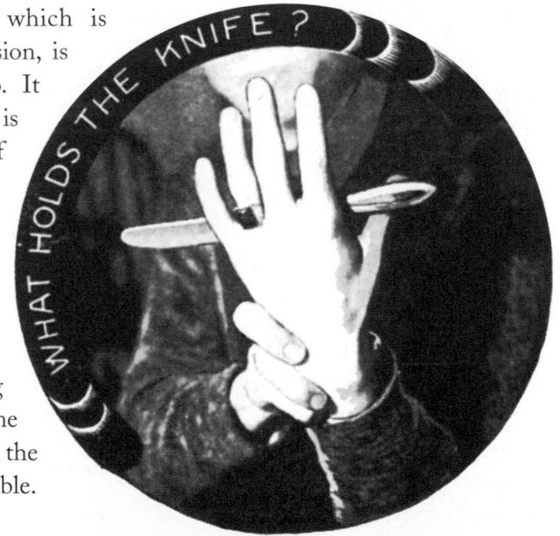

Optical Illusions

— The Wrong-Size Cardboard Segments —

Two identical segments cut from a 20 in. cardboard ring, as indicated by the black portions in the lower detail, will not appear to be the same size when laid down next to each other on a table and viewed from the position indicated. The effect that results was reproduced by taking a photo from a position behind and above the head of the figure. In analyzing the illusion, there is the natural effect of the closer segment appearing larger, to both eye and camera, but this effect is accentuated by the angles and curves of the arrangement.

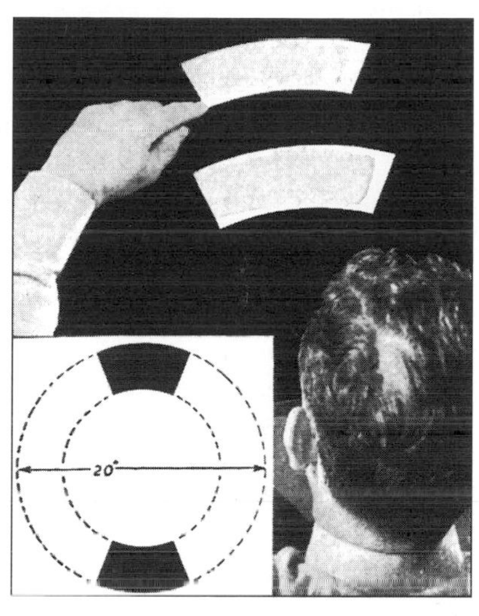

Which piece is larger?

— A Simple Optical Illusion —

The engraving shows a perfectly straight boxwood rule laid over a number of turned brass rings of various sizes. Although the effect in the illustration is less pronounced than it

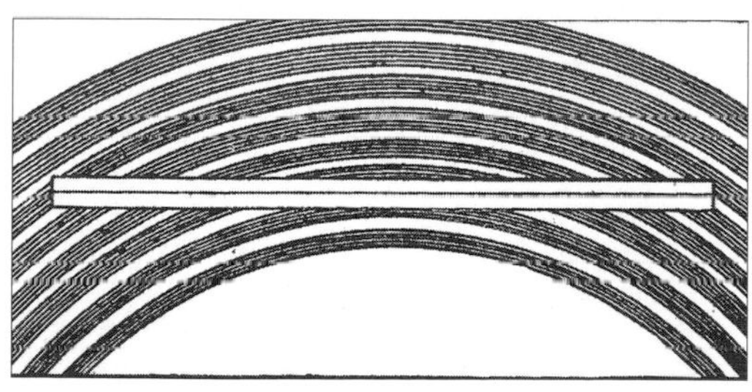

A Bent rule?

is in reality, it will be noticed that the rule appears to be bent. But sighting along the rule from one end will show that it is perfectly straight.

The brass rings also appear distorted. The portions on one side of the rule do not appear to be a continuation of those on the other, but that they really are can be proved by sighting in the same manner as before.

— A Lively Optical Illusion —

When looking at the accompanying sketch, you will say that the letters are alternately inclined to the right and left. They are not so, however, and this can be proved by measuring the distance of the top and bottom of any vertical strokes from the edge of the entire block: they will be found to be exactly the same distance. Or take any of the horizontal strokes of the four letters and see how far their extremities are from the top and bottom of the entire block. It will be found that a line joining the extremities of the strokes is strictly parallel to the top or bottom, and that they are not on a slant at all. It is the slant of the numerous short lines making up the letter as a whole that deceives the eye.

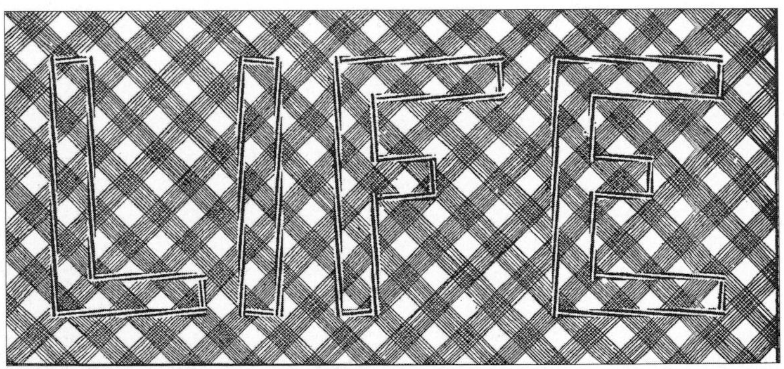

Is life slanted?

— The Spiral-Cord Illusion —

After taking a look at the accompanying illustration, you will be positive that the cords shown run in a spiral toward the center—yet it really shows a series of perfect circles of cords placed one inside the other. You can test this for yourself in a moment with a pair of compasses or, still more simply, by laying the point of a pencil on any part of the cord and following it round. Instead of approaching or receding from the center in a continuous line, as in the case of a spiral, you will find the pencil returning to the point from which it started.

THE CORD IS NOT A SPIRAL.

— The Two Circles Illusion —

The accompanying sketch shows two optical illusions. The first, having a perfect circle on the outside edge, appears to be flattened at the points, *A*, while the arcs of the circle, *B*, appear to be more rounding. In the second figure, the circle appears to have an oval form, with the distance from *C* to *C* greater than from *D* to *D*. A compass applied to the circles in either figures will show they are perfectly round.

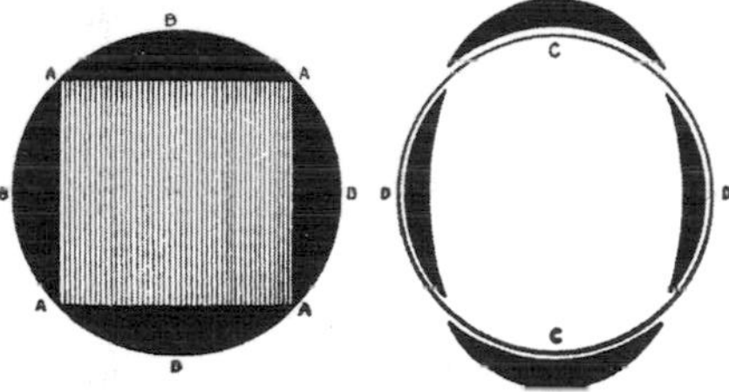

{CHAPTER 5}

THE MAGIC *of* SCIENCE

ENCHANTED CHEMISTRY

— THE GHOST SUGAR —

In this effect, the performer drops a lump of sugar into his coffee. It sinks to the bottom of the cup immediately, and in a manner thoroughly unmagical. But wait! Presently the sugar bobs up to the surface, where it floats around buoyantly and smiles sarcastically at an amazed audience.

THE MYSTICAL FLOATING LUMP OF SUGAR

The chemical agent in this effect is that simple preparation called collodion. The sugar is previously dipped into this solution. This must be done rapidly, and the sugar should be held there for only an instant. After the dipping, the sugar should be allowed to dry for about twenty-four hours.

The prepared lump will sink instantly when dropped into the coffee. But as the sugar rapidly dissolves, the framework of collodion will presently bob up on the surface of the coffee. The collodion lump should not be left about, for its appearance is quite like any other lump of sugar, and someone might—oh, well!

— The Levitating Mothball —

The performer exhibits an ordinary mothball. He drops the ball into a glass of water. It sinks. Then, on the command of the performer, the mothball rises to the surface of the water. On a further command, it goes to the bottom again, then finally returns to the top, where it is removed by the magician and passed around for inspection.

Really, there's nothing to it. The mothball is simply a mothball. The water is carbonated water procured from the corner drugstore.

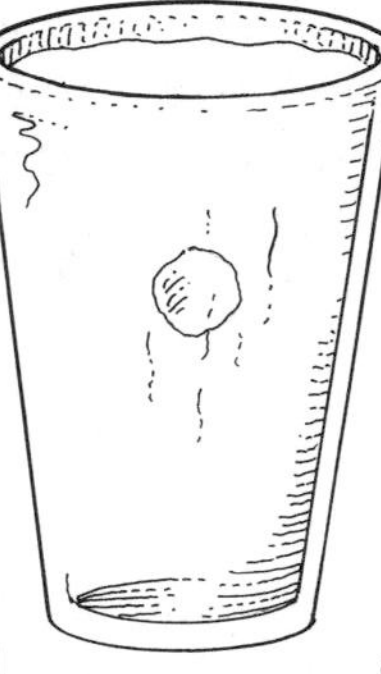

A MOTHBALL THAT MOVES ON COMMAND

When the mothball is dropped into the water, it naturally sinks to the bottom. At the bottom of the glass, however, it breathes gas from the carbonated water and presently becomes light enough to bob its way to the surface, only to sink again as the gas escapes. The magician need only time his commands in a test run to synchronize with the chemical reaction—and there you are!

— The Magic Candle —

Did you ever happen to hear the story about the girl and the magic candle? Well, the candle went out and left the girl in fearsome darkness. "Oh, dear me," she wailed, "what'll I do?" And then she remembered a fairy story, and, touching the candle wick to the edge of a glass of water she was carrying to her sick grandmother, she got her flame back again—no fooling!

That last is the patter; the actual

trick is done with a small piece of phosphorus, about the size of a pinhead. This is stuck to the rim of the glass with a minute piece of tallow. When the hot wick of the candle touches the phosphorus, it ignites immediately and lights the candle. At the instant of the lighting, the tumbler should be tilted so that the candle appears to be lit again from contact with the water.

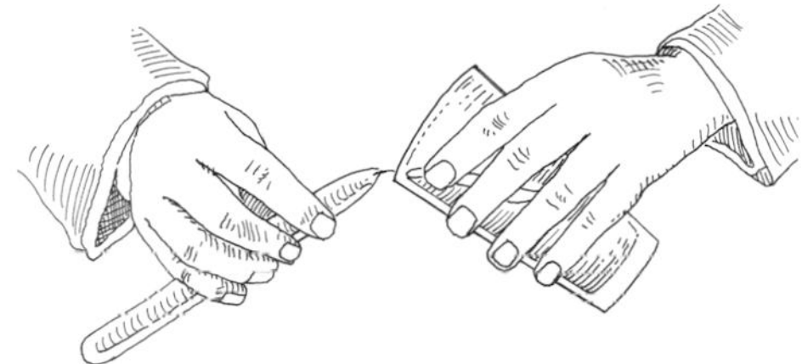

LIGHTING A CANDLE WITH THE EDGE OF A WATER GLASS

Phosphorus, by the way, should be kept moist when not in use, because it ignites with extraordinary quickness at a comparatively low temperature.

— WATER-AND-WINE TRICK —

This is an interesting trick based on the chemical properties of acids and alkalies. The materials needed are one glass pitcher filled with water, four glass tumblers, and an acid, an alkali, and some phenolphthalein solution that can be obtained from your local druggist. Before the performance, add a few drops of the phenolphthalein to the water in the pitcher and rub a small quantity of the alkali solution on the sides of two of the tumblers, then repeat, using only as large a quantity of the acid as will escape notice on the remaining tumblers.

Set the tumblers so that you will know which is which. Hold a prepared tumbler with the left hand and pour some of the liquid from the pitcher, which is held in the right hand. The liquid poured into the glass will turn red like wine. Set this full tumbler aside, take the pitcher in the left hand, and pour some of the liquid into one of the tumblers containing the acid, as the tumbler is held in the right hand. There will be no change in color. Repeat both parts in the same order, then begin to pour the liquids contained in the tumblers back into the pitcher in reverse order; the excess of acid will neutralize the alkali and cause it to lose its color. In the end, the pitcher will contain a colorless liquid.

— Burning Sugar —

The average person imagines that lump sugar, being almost pure carbon, will burn readily. But the fact is that it does nothing of the kind; it merely melts away when a lit match is held under it. Of course, if you are a magician—well, you know how clever some people really are!

The secret is simple: The sugar must be previously rubbed casually into some cigarette ash. The ash, adhering to the lump, will give it sufficient "timber" to burn readily.

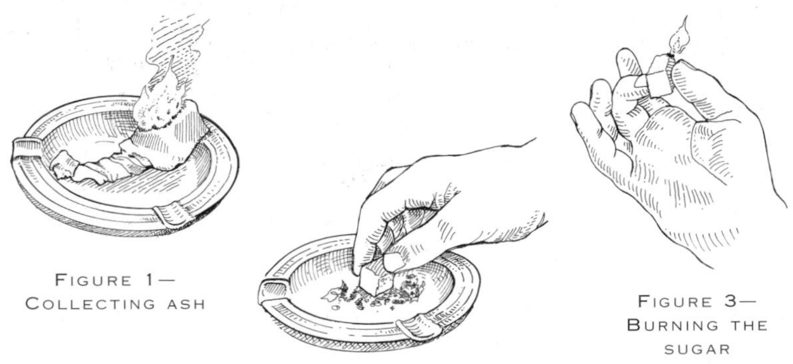

Figure 1—Collecting ash

Figure 2—Lightly rubbing the sugar in ash

Figure 3—Burning the sugar

— Fire from Ice —

In this trick, the performer demonstrates just how convenient it is to be possessed of the magical touch. With no matches available, the magician lights his cigarette from a piece of ice that he has removed from a glass of iced tea. How's that for service?

Of course, no one is supposed to know that his cigarette was previously treated, with a small bit of potassium inserted in one end. When the potassium comes in contact with the wet ice, it instantly ignites and lights the cigarette. Be sure you know which end of the cigarette is which, before you proceed with the nonchalant gesture.

Numerical Possibilities

— Bewitched-Cube Puzzle —

This simple puzzle, which requires six numbered cubes, will take considerable concentration to make it come out right. Six wooden cubes are provided and numbered on each of their six faces from 1 to 6, the order of numbering being different for each cube, as shown in *Figures 1* and *2.*

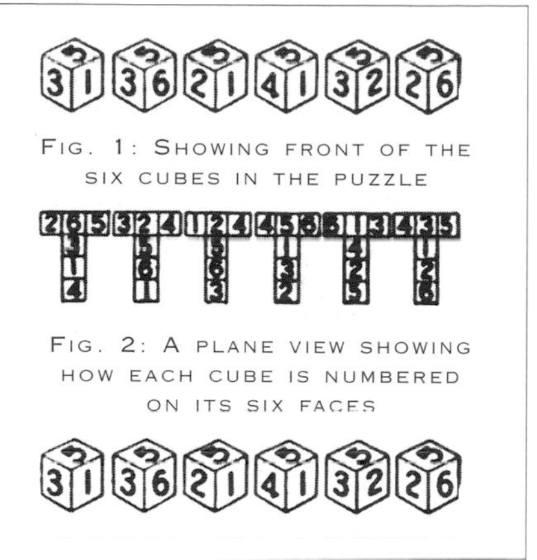

Fig. 1: Showing front of the six cubes in the puzzle

Fig. 2: A plane view showing how each cube is numbered on its six faces

The object is to arrange the six cubes in any shape—preferably in a straight line—as in *Figure 3,* so that the figures 1, 2, 3, 4, 5, and 6 will appear at once on the top, bottom, front, back, and right- and left-hand faces. They will not be in consecutive order, but the six numbers must each show from every side. Separating the cubes slightly will show the right- and left-hand faces. Once this is properly arranged, the blocks may be transposed hundreds of different ways in a straight line, fulfilling the conditions each time.

— The Age-Revealing Trick —

A wonderful trick with numbers involves telling a person's age and his street number by a series of commands. The person writes his street number on a sheet of paper shielded from the magician's gaze. His next command is to double it, add five, and multiply the total by fifty. To this amount he adds his age. The last command is to add the number of days in a year to his total and subtract 615. The last figures will be his age, the others his house number.

— Magic Numbers —

An interesting paper-tearing trick starts with a magician displaying a sheet of paper on which the numbers 1, 2, 3, and 4 have been inscribed, from left to right, and underneath them, from right to left, 5, 6, 7, and 8. By a series of folds, the sheet is reduced to a triangle. The performer explains that he will, at

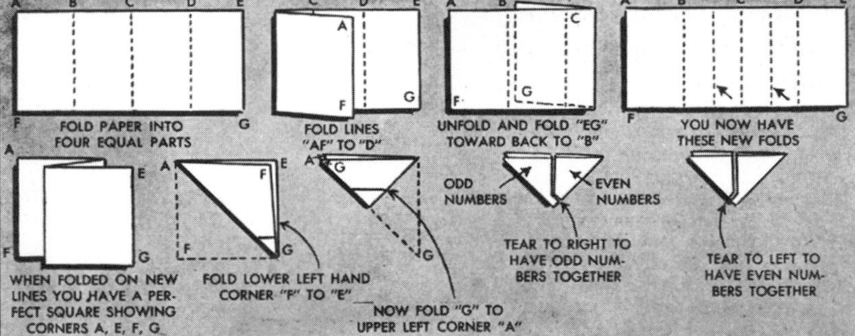

a spectator's bidding, make a single tear in the triangle so that only the odd or the even numbers will be left on the paper.

Write the numbers on a slip of paper, fold it as shown, and with a single tear down the center of the triangle, odd or even numbers are left together.

Physical Artifice

— The Thousand-Pound Newspaper —

For this surprising trick, you'll need two sheets of newspaper without holes or tears, a slat from a wooden apple or orange crate, and a baseball bat.

Instruct the spectators that—for a moment only—you will make the weight of a plain, ordinary newspaper increase a hundredfold. And the trick shall be to prove that claim.

Lay the wooden slat on a table, with ¼ of the length projecting out over the end of the table. Now cover it with several sheets of newspaper. Carefully smooth out the newspaper all over the table, so that it lies absolutely flat.

Pick up the baseball bat and raise it, saying your magic words at the same time. Bring it down hard on the projecting piece of slat. Instead of the paper and slat flying off the table, as any reasonable spectator would expect, the slat will break right in two at the edge of the table.

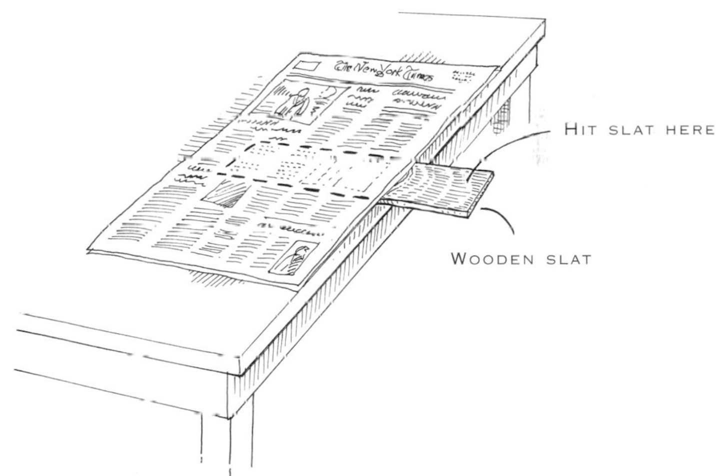

Instead of flying off the table when struck, the slat breaks in two.

Here's the secret: As you know by preparing this trick, air is pushing down on top of the newspaper. Even though the newspaper is lying flat on the table, there is still air pushing up between it and the table. If you push down slowly on the slat instead of hitting it with the bat, the other end of it and the newspaper will rise, because the air has a chance to flow in under the newspaper and push up under the slat. But when you come down hard with the baseball bat, the other end starts to go up fast. That little bit of air underneath expands until it's very, very thin—almost nothing, in fact. It can't push very hard compared to the air on top of the paper pushing down. None of the air on the outside can get in to help that thin air push up, because the newspaper prevents the air from getting in for even a fraction of a second. So the weight of the whole column of air above the newspaper holds that end of the slat down tight, with about the same force as if there were a thousand pounds of coal piled up there! With all the pressure on one end of the slat and you hitting the other end with a baseball bat, there's no mystery (at least to you) about why it breaks in two!

— The Phantom Ink Well —

This easy little trick calls for nothing more than a sheet of writing paper, an empty fountain pen, a lemon, and a lamp. Cut the lemon in half, and you have your "phantom ink well." Dip the fountain pen in the lemon and write the words "I hate the light" on a plain white sheet of paper.

Ghost-writing

During the performance, the magician must create a tension-filled presentation with a story about a ghost that haunts the house, coming out after dark and terrifying all he can find there. The magician should explain that he has a correspondence with the ghost, who writes with his special Phantom Ink Well.

Now hold the paper you've written on close in front of a small lamp; as the audience looks on, the words slowly appear. To make an even greater impact, use a lamp with a cord switch that you can bump with your knee, extinguishing the lights just as the message becomes apparent and raising the level of fright even higher!

— The Fireproof Coin —

Tell your audience you have a magic coin that can stop fabric from burning. Place the coin inside a handkerchief, wrapping the handkerchief tightly over the surface of the coin. Now take a lit cigarette and place the burning end against the covered surface of the coin. The handkerchief will not burn.

To prove it is not a specially treated handkerchief, remove the coin and burn a hole in the handkerchief with the cigarette; it should burn quickly and easily. The difference is the metal of the coin, which conducts the heat so quickly that the fabric doesn't have a chance to get hot enough to burn.

— The Fingertip of Sound —

Another modest trick that will never fail to entertain requires only a tumbler and a fork. Announce to your friends that you can carry sound in your fingertip. Casually conceal your left hand, with the fork in it, below the table level. Rap the fork against the underside of the table, touching the handle with your fingertips. Bring the fingertip of your right forefinger to the rim of the glass and, as you touch the glass, touch the fork handle secretly to the underside of the table. The audience will hear a musical note that seems to come from the glass!

— Magic Fire Extinguisher —

This is a nifty little dinner-table trick that may not make an act all by itself but is very entertaining anyway. The performer tells his companions that he can create a magic invisible force that will extinguish flame. Intrigued, the dining companions watch as the performer folds a piece of paper in half lengthwise, then adds a teaspoon of baking soda to a glass of water that is a little less than half full (*Figure 1*). Place a saucer or a piece of cardboard on top of the glass for a minute or so (*Figure 2*) and then perform the stunt.

Holding the paper up so that the fold makes a trough leading to the candle flame (*Figure 3*), the performer tips the glass as if pouring liquid into the top of the trough, without actually spilling out any of the contents of the glass (*Figure 4*). The candle goes out, and dining companions are suitably impressed.

The skill is more chemical than magical: you've shut off the supply of oxygen from around the candle flame by pouring carbon dioxide on it, thus extinguishing the flame.

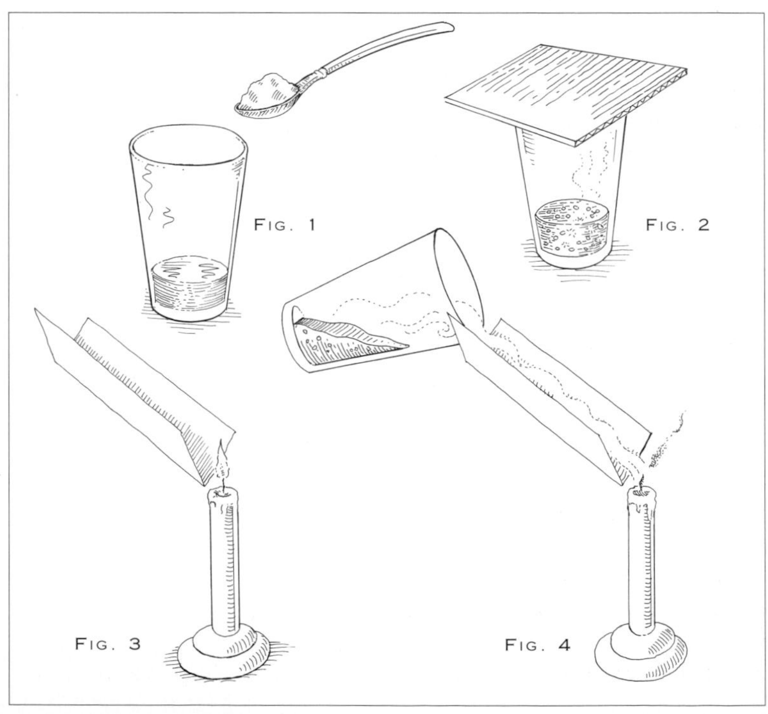

— Pencil Glue —

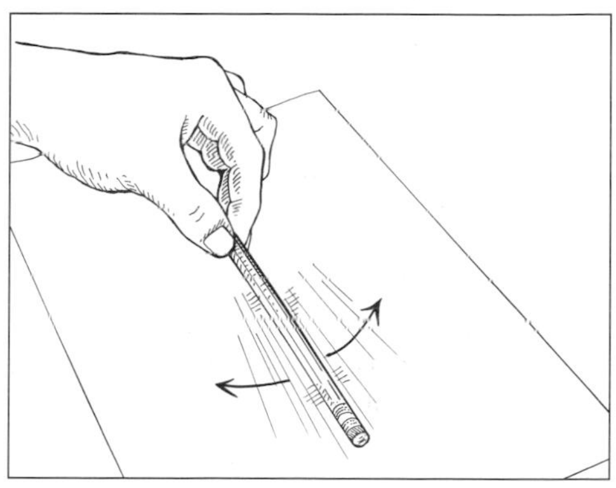

Rubbing a pencil across a piece of paper to prepare it for sticking to the wall

A neat little party trick that you can produce just about anywhere, this works with just a pencil and a piece of paper. Promise the spectator that you can stick a piece of paper to the wall without the aid of any adhesive. When the person displays disbelief, prove it by simply rubbing the pencil back and forth over the paper, as shown

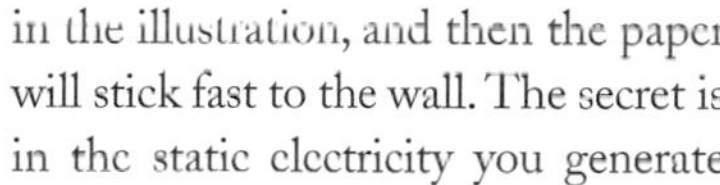

in the illustration, and then the paper will stick fast to the wall. The secret is in the static electricity you generate with the pencil, which makes the paper grab tight to the wall better than any horse glue ever could.

— Making a Coin Stick to Wood —

Take a quarter and place it flat against a vertical surface of wood, such as the side of a bookcase, door facing, or door panel, then strike it hard with a downward sliding motion, pressing it against the wood. Take the hand away, and the coin will remain on the woodwork. The striking and pressure expel the air between the quarter and the wood, thus forming a vacuum sufficient to hold the coin.

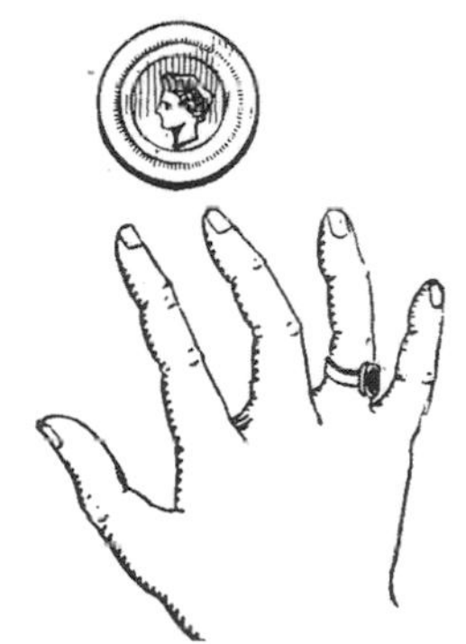

The coin sticks on a vertical surface.

— Cutting a Thread Inside a Glass Bottle—

This is a trick that can be performed only when the sun shines, but it is a good one. Procure a clear glass bottle and stick a pin in the lower end of the cork. Attach a thread to the pin and tie a small weight to the end of the thread, so it will hang inside the bottle when the cork is in place. Inform your audience that you will sever the thread and cause the weight to drop without removing the cork.

The glass directs the sun's rays.

All that is required to perform the feat is to hold a magnifying glass so as to direct the sun's rays onto the thread. The thread will quickly burn, and the weight will fall.

{CHAPTER 6}

MONEY MYSTIFICATION

Disappearing Denominations

— The Paper Fold and Disappearing Coin

This impromptu little trick will often cause much wonderment. A piece of paper, about 6 or 8 in. square, is shown, free from preparation. A fifty-cent piece is placed in the middle of it, and one side of the paper folded down so as to cover the coin, which may now be felt inside the paper. One side of the paper is now folded down, then the other side, with the audience feeling the coin in the paper each time. The fourth side is finally folded over—when, lo and behold! The coin is found to have disappeared; it is no longer in the paper, which is promptly torn up. It then may be produced from a gentleman's pocket, or wherever desired.

The secret of this trick consists of the folding of the paper. If the reader

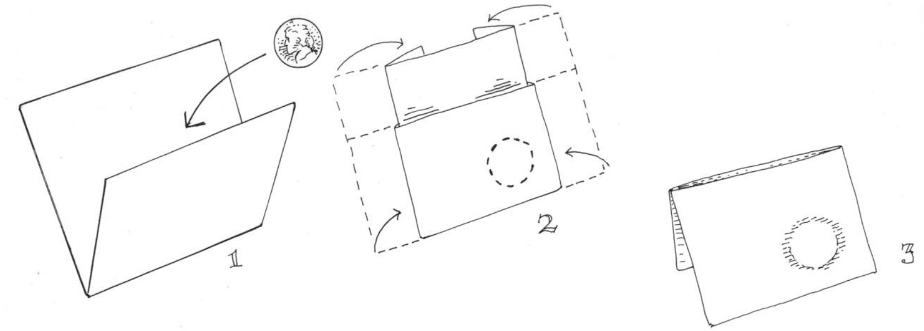

THE PROPER METHOD FOR FOLDING THE PAPER

will experiment, he will see that the first three folds are genuine, really serving to enclose the coin. But as the fourth side is folded down so as to contain the coin, the paper is tilted up and the coin allowed to fall into the lower space. It will now be found that the coin, instead of being actually folded into the paper, is contained in a sort of loose pocket; if the paper is then tilted up, the coin will slide out, into the palm of the hand—where it can be palmed, to be produced again later as the performer sees fit. The folded paper is immediately torn up to prevent inspection, which would reveal the secret at once.

— THE DISAPPEARING-COIN TRICK —

Here's a trick for the next party: A coin is wrapped inside three small sheets of paper, one over the other. Then, while keeping the wrapped coin before your eyes, the performer shows how the coin is wrapped. Next, he lays the paper on the table and unwraps it in full view of the spectators—who discover that the coin has disappeared.

And now to explain. Prepare by cutting seven squares of colored paper to the dimensions shown—two yellow, two pink, and two green (*Figure 1*). The last and largest one is white paper (*Figure 2*). Crease the sheets to fold as indicated, place the two green sheets back to back, and glue the center panels together (*Figures 3* and *4*). Place the green sheets on the table, with one pink and one yellow sheet on top, and fold

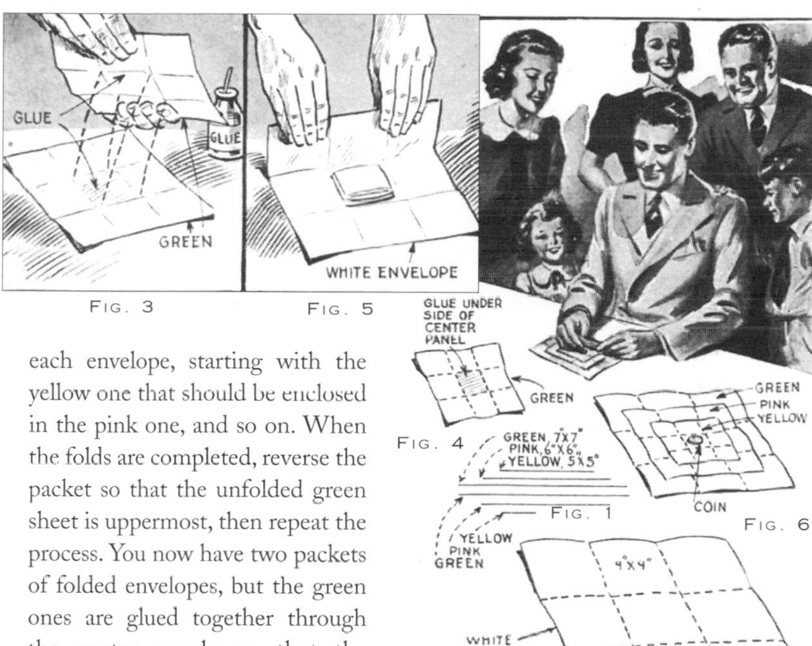

FIG. 3

FIG. 5

FIG. 4

FIG. 1

FIG. 6

FIG. 2

each envelope, starting with the yellow one that should be enclosed in the pink one, and so on. When the folds are completed, reverse the packet so that the unfolded green sheet is uppermost, then repeat the process. You now have two packets of folded envelopes, but the green ones are glued together through the center panels, so that the assembly appears as one package. With this enclosed in the white envelope (*Figure 5*), you are ready for the performance. Placing the packet on the table, borrow a coin. Ask the donor to observe the date on the coin's face.

Unwrapping the envelopes and leaving them in the order shown, place the coin in the center of the smallest envelope and refold them separately as before (*Figure 6*). But before finishing by enclosing them in the white envelope, give the green packet an extra turn that will bring the empty assembly of envelopes uppermost. This extra flip of the package will not be noticed, as your folding is accomplished by turning each envelope over in its turn. Now unfold the sheets. The last and yellow envelope will be found empty. To make the coin reappear, refold the envelopes and repeat the turning of packet after the green one is closed.

— A New Coin Vanish —

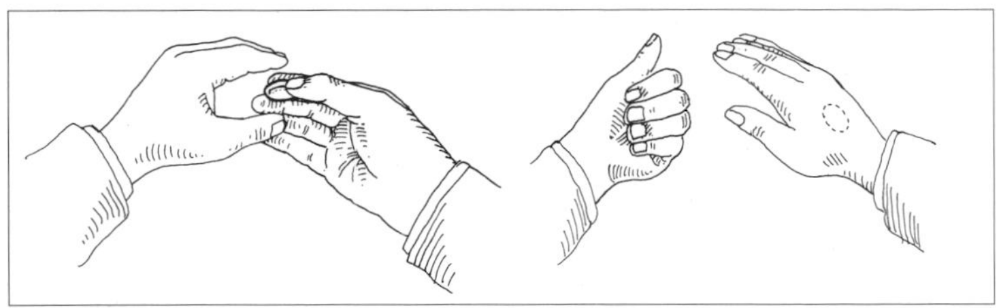

Another palming trick

A coin is shown, held in the right hand between the thumb and second finger. The left hand is held open, palm upward, and the coin is fairly placed in the center of the palm, with the fingers closed around it. The right hand does not release the coin or change its position, until the left hand is slowly turned over and around the coin—which then "makes its exit" through the side of the hand near the thumb. The left hand now covers the coin, which, with the aid of the first and second fingers of the right hand, is quickly drawn up to the base of the thumb, where it is "thumb-palmed." The right hand now pulls up the left sleeve, at the same time dropping the coin into the breast pocket of the coat. The coin has now "vanished."

— The Missing Quarter —

While this is purely a sleight-of-hand trick, it will take very little practice to cause the coin to disappear instantly. Take a quarter between the thumb and finger, as shown, and whirl the coin with a rapid twist of the fingers, at the same time closing the hand; the coin will disappear up your coat sleeve. On opening the hand, the coin will not be seen. Take three quarters and hold one in the palm of the left hand. Place one between the thumb and finger of each hand, then give the coin in the

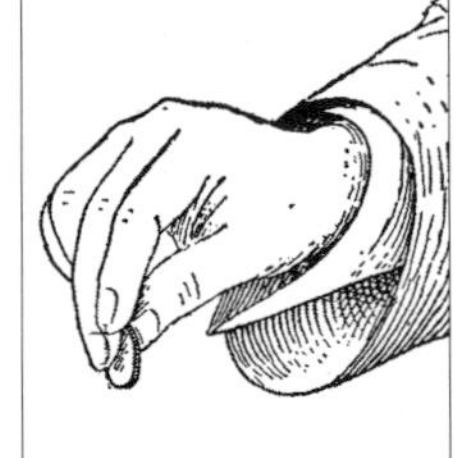

right hand a whirl, as described, closing both hands quickly. The coin in the right hand will disappear (up your sleeve), while the left hand, on being unclosed, will contain two quarters.

Toll Collectors

— Dropping Coins in a Glass Full of Water —

Take a glass, place it on a table, and fill it to the brim with water, taking care that the surface of the water is raised a little above the edge of the glass, but not running over. Place a number of nickels or dimes on the table near the glass, then ask your spectators how many coins can be put into the water without making it overflow. No doubt the reply will be that the water will run over before even two coins are dropped in. But it is possible to put in ten or twelve of them. With a great deal of care, the coins may be made to fall without disturbing the water, the surface of which will become more and more convex before the water overflows.

— Catching Coins in a Wineglass —

This trick is performed with the aid of an ordinary large-sized, long-stemmed claret glass, which can be freely passed around for scrutiny and examination. Then the performer walks round the room or stage, holding this glass out at arm's length from him, with the other hand down at his side. The audience then both hears and sees coins, coming apparently out of thin air, fall into the glass. The explanation is very simple: The performer shows his right hand to be empty and with his left picks up the claret glass, showing it to be an ordinary glass,

OUTSIDE VIEW INSIDE VIEW

without guile! While doing this, however, he lets his right hand drop to his servante and picks up a stack of coins that he had previously placed there. He palms them, and when he has finished showing the glass with his left hand, he passes it to his right. The middle finger of the right hand then grips the stem of the glass, and the coins are palmed in such a way that they rest on the third joint of the third finger—the knuckle of which rests on the stand of the glass (see illustration).

— TAKING A DOLLAR BILL FROM AN APPLE —

A rather pleasing, yet puzzling, deception is to pass a dollar bill into the interior of an examined lemon or apple. This can be accomplished in several ways, either mechanically or purely by sleight of hand. The mechanical method, of course, is easier and really just as effective. In performing this trick, a plate with three apples is first exhibited, and the audience is given a choice of any one of them for use in the experiment. The selected one is tossed around for examination and then returned to the performer, who places it in full view of the spectators while he makes the dollar bill vanish (see illustration). Taking the knife, he cuts the apple into two pieces, requesting the audience to select one of them. Squeezing this piece, he extracts the dollar bill.

The entire secret is in the unsuspected article—the table knife. The knife is prepared by boring out the wooden handle to make it hollow.

THE DOLLAR BILL IS HIDDEN IN THE KNIFE HANDLE THAT CUTS THE APPLE.

Enough space must be made to hold a dollar bill. The knife lies on the table with the fruit, the open end facing the performer. After the bill has been made to vanish and the examined apple returned to the entertainer, he takes the fruit and cuts it in half. One of the halves is chosen, and the performer impales it on the end of the knife blade and holds it out for the audience to view it. While still holding the knife, he turns the blade downward, grasps the half of an apple, and crushes it with a slight pass toward the end of the knife handle, where the bill is grasped along with the apple—which results in a perfect illusion of taking the bill out of the apple.

As to the disappearance of the dollar bill, there are many ways in which this may be accomplished. Perhaps the method requiring the least practice is to place the bill in the trouser pocket, then show the audience that the pocket is empty. This can be done by rolling the bill into a small compass and pushing it into the extreme upper corner of the pocket, where it will remain undetected while the pocket is pulled out for inspection. Other combinations can be arranged with the use of the knife, which is simple to make and very inexpensive.

— One Dime into Three —

Procure, if possible, three dimes of the same date and approximately in the same state of wear. Stick two of these to the underside of the table by means of wax, about ½ in. from the edge. The coins must be several inches apart. Then turn up your sleeves, take the third dime in the right hand, and draw particular attention to its date and general appearance and, indirectly, to the fact that you have no other coin concealed in your hands. Turn back the table cover and rub the dime backward and forward on the edge of the table. In this position, while rubbing with the thumb, the fingers will be brought underneath the table edge and consequently will be able to touch the other dimes. After rubbing a few seconds, pull away your hand with a quick jerk, carrying away with it one of the concealed dimes, which you then exhibit as having been produced by friction. Pocketing the waxed dime, repeat the operation with the remaining dime.

— Find the Coin —

This is an uncommon trick, entirely homemade, yet the results are as startling as in many of the professional tricks. A small baking-powder can is employed to vanish the coin, which should be marked by one of the audience for identification. Cut a slot in the bottom on the side of the can, as shown in *Figure 1.* This slot should be just large enough for the coin that is used to pass through freely, as well as to have its lower edge at a level with the bottom of the can.

The series of boxes in which the coin is next found should consist of four small-sized, flat pasteboard boxes, square or rectangular shaped and furnished with hinged covers. The smallest need be no larger than necessary to hold the coin, and each succeeding box should be just large enough to hold the next smaller one, which in turn will contain the others.

A strip of tin about 1 by 1¾ in. is bent in the shape shown in *Figure 2* to serve as a guide for the coin through the various boxes. This guide is inserted about ⅛ in. in the smallest box, between the cover and the box, and three rubber bands are wrapped around the box as indicated. This box is then enclosed in the next larger box, the guide being allowed to project between the box and the cover, and the necessary tension is secured by three rubber bands around the box as before. In like manner, the remaining boxes are adjusted so that finally the prepared nest of boxes appears as in *Figure 3.*

The coin can easily be passed into the inner box through the tin guide and then the guide can be

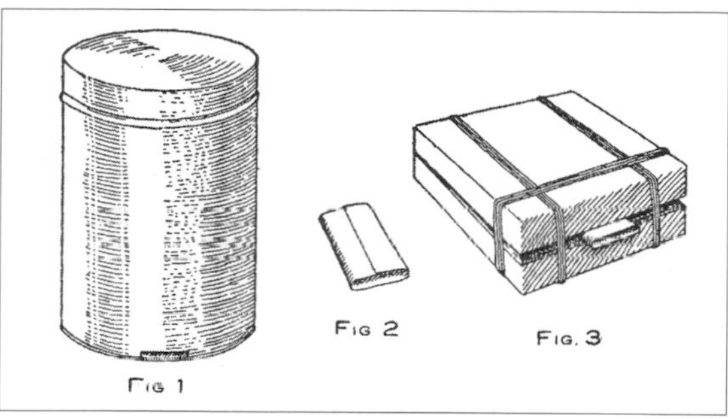

APPLIANCES FOR THE DISAPPEARING COIN

withdrawn, which permits the respective boxes to close and the rubber bands to hold each one in a closed position.

The performer comes forward with the tin can in his right hand, the bottom of the can in his palm with the slot at the right side. He removes the cover with the left hand and passes his wand around the inner part of the can, which is then turned upside down to prove that it contains nothing. The marked coin is dropped into the can by someone in the audience. The cover is replaced and the can shaken, so the coin will rattle within. The shaking of the can is continued until the coin has slipped through the slot into his palm. The can is then placed on the table with the performer's left hand.

Then he apparently looks for something to cover the can. This is found to be a handkerchief, which was previously prepared on another table concealing the nest of boxes. The coin in the right hand is quickly slipped into the guide of the nest of boxes, which was placed in an upright position, and the guide is withdrawn and dropped on the table. The performer, while doing this, is explaining that he is looking for a suitable cover for the can, but as he cannot find one he takes the handkerchief instead. The handkerchief is spread over the can, and then he brings the nest of boxes. He explains how he will transfer the coin, then passes his wand from the can to the boxes. The can is then shown to be empty and the boxes given to someone in the audience to be opened. The spectators will be greatly surprised to find the marked coin within the innermost box.

— The Coin-and-Hat Trick —

Two borrowed hats are set side by side on the table, and the performer makes two marked fifty-cent pieces pass invisibly from one to the other, in this manner: Take the two coins in the right hand and pretend to pass them into the left, while actually palming them in the right. The left hand must now, as heretofore, be kept closed. Pick up one of the hats with the right hand, fingers inside and thumb out, thus bringing the two coins against the lining of the hat. Retain them there by the pressure of the fingers. The interior of the hat may now be shown as empty, after which the hat is placed on the table, crown downward.

At the same moment, extend the left hand, still closed, and to all appearances containing the coins, over the second hat. Open your hand as if releasing the coins, at the same time dropping the coins concealed in the right hand into the hat held in the right hand. The audience hears the jingle at that moment and believes that you have dropped them into the other hat. After a proper interval, and with sufficient ceremony, announce that you have caused them to change their location. Then exhibit the two coins from the supposedly empty hat. The spectators are, as a rule, thoroughly impressed.

— The Magic Coin Tray —

The following is an excellent little trick when well performed. The performer brings forward a small tin tray, about 4 x 6 in. square, in which rest twelve pennies. The performer asks someone in the audience to step up onstage and assist him in this trick. A volunteer having been procured, the performer seats him in a convenient chair. This new assistant is asked to remove the coins from the tray, then count them one by one, so that the audience can see exactly how many coins there are. Twelve coins are counted. The performer then asks his assistant to remove four of the coins and give them to him. Eight coins then remain in the tray. The assistant is asked to place his two hands together in the form of a cup, and into this cup the performer pours the

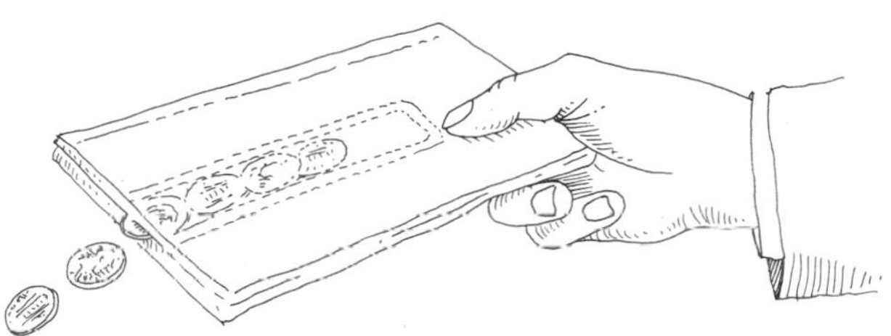

The tray's secret slot

eight coins remaining in the tray. The assistant is then asked to close his hands tightly, so that it would be impossible for the magician either to extract or to add to any of the coins in his hands. Meanwhile, the remaining four pennies are seen to be in the performer's left hand.

An empty glass is now shown and may be examined by the audience. It is then placed on the performer's table. Seemingly shifting the four coins to his right hand, the performer drops them into the glass, and they may be distinctly heard by the audience as they fall into the tumbler. The performer instantly seizes the glass in his two hands, holding the mouth of it in one palm and the base in the other, then rapidly advances toward his assistant. Reaching him, the performer pronounces the mystic words, "One, two, three! Pass!" The glass is instantly shown to be empty. The coins have vanished—they are no longer in the glass or in the performer's hands. The volunteer is then requested to count out into the tray the number of coins in his hands. On his counting them separately, it is found that he now has twelve coins, the original number. Such is the effect of the trick on an audience. Now for the explanation.

In fact, sixteen coins are used for the performance of this trick. At the outset, twelve of these rest on the surface of the tray, which is of special construction. The remaining four are hidden in a groove that runs along the underside of the tray, between the top and bottom, so that they are invisible, no matter which side of the tray is seen. Four coins are removed, but when the volunteer assistant's hands are held together and the plate tipped up so as to allow the eight coins resting on its surface to run into the assistant's hands, the four coins under the tray will also pass into his hands—so that he is holding twelve coins from the outset (see illustration). He cannot detect this, however, because, owing to the relatively large number of coins, he cannot tell exactly how many coins he is holding before he closes his hands over them as instructed by the performer. The mystery of the first part of the trick is thus explained.

Now for the magical disappearance from the performer's hands. Taking four pennies in the fingertips of his left hand, he brings the right hand toward them. He pretends to take them in the right hand—but in reality leaves them in the palm of the left, a technique known as the *tourniquet* or French drop. The right hand is immediately closed and moved away from the left hand, the eyes of the performer following it, as though it really contained the four coins. The closed right hand approaches the glass on the table, assumes a position immediately over it, extends the fingers, and makes the motion of dropping the coins into the glass.

The illusion of the sound is caused in this manner: The performer has a second tumbler on his servante. Into this he drops the four coins from his left hand, which he has allowed to drop idly behind the table while looking at the outstretched right hand. At the moment the fingers of the right hand open, the four coins are dropped from the left hand into the second glass. The spectators, hearing this, come to the conclusion that the coins are really being deposited in the glass on the table. In order that the spectators may not see that no coins are in the visible glass, this should be fluted or cut for 2 or 3 in. up from the base. In this way, from a little distance, it is impossible to tell whether the glass is in fact empty. This, well executed, is a highly effective trick.

Change Change

— The Heads-and-Tails Trick —

This little sleight is a very original trick. The performer borrows a coin and "flicks" it into the air, as he normally would to cause it to come down "heads or tails." It is caught by the right hand and placed on the back of the (closed) left hand, outstretched for the purpose. The right hand is removed, showing the coin.

The performer does this once or twice, saying meanwhile, "Now, if anyone guesses correctly this time, they can have the coin!" The same action is apparently gone through, when a cry of "Heads!" (let us say) is made. The performer then removes his right hand—whereupon the coin will be found to have vanished altogether!

The explanation lies in the fact that as the magician's right hand dips downward for the final "flip" after two or three preliminary tosses into the air, he drops the coin into the left hand, waiting to receive it. The right hand is then closed as if the coin is in it again, brought upward with the performer's eyes following it, retained in the air for a moment, and placed, opened, onto the back of the left hand. When the right hand is removed, the coin is seen to have vanished; afterward it can be made to appear, if desired, in the left hand.

Thus described, the trick may appear too simple and obvious to prove effective, but it is nevertheless one of the most effective sleights in existence. When well done, it will prove baffling even to your magical friends, when shown for the first time.

— The Multiplying Half-Dollar —

This very pretty little illusion is really an optical trick, depending on the line of vision of your audience for its success. The effect of the trick is that the magician, after showing a single half-dollar in his fingertips and exhibiting all sides of it (to prove that only one half-dollar is really there), suddenly causes it to become two.

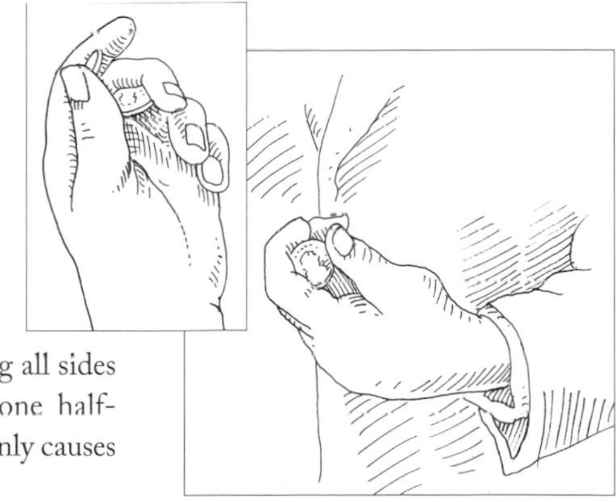

The secret consists of the fact that, while one half-dollar is held in a vertical position, another coin is concealed behind it. This coin is held by the thumb and forefinger in a horizontal position. By turning the hand around, all sides and the edge of the coin may be shown, thus proving its "singleness." Care must be taken, however, to hold the coin so that the second (horizontal) one is concealed by the thumb and forefinger of the hand. If care is taken to study the eyeline of the onlookers, this may be accomplished successfully. After showing all sides in this manner, the performer merely has to "clink" the two coins together and throw them on the table, where they may be examined.

— The Flying Coins —

The performer counts out twelve coins on his table and asks someone in the company to act as his assistant. The assistant having been found, the performer gives him four coins and cautions him to hold them tightly. The performer himself then takes eight coins and, holding them above his head, commands four of them to appear in the hands of the volunteer. On examination, this is found to have happened, for the performer now holds only four coins and the assistant is tightly grasping eight. Next, the assistant is given eight to hold, with the performer taking the remaining four. After the performer says, "Presto, change!" the volunteer finds to his amazement that the performer's hands are empty and that he, the volunteer, holds the entire dozen!

To achieve this, the performer must be provided with sixteen coins, all alike. Four of these the performer has palmed in his right hand at the commencement of the trick. After elaborately counting out the four that the assistant is to hold, he takes them all in his right hand, adding at the same time the four coins originally palmed, thereby making eight. He now picks up the remaining eight coins from the table, and apparently transfers them from the right hand into the left, but in reality transfers only four. The mystic "pass" is then pronounced, and the first part of the trick is done.

The second part is just a repetition of the first. You secretly add four palmed coins to the eight that you pretend to hand to the assistant, telling him at the same time to make doubly sure this time, and so engage his attention until his hands are closed. In transferring the coins from the right hand to the left, the "pass" is used. The left hand is drawn away closed, while the coins remain in the right. The incantation is pronounced, the performer's hand is shown to be empty, and the assistant finds he has all twelve coins in his possession.

— The Coin-and-Card Trick —

The following is a combination coin-and-card trick. Two cards are drawn from the pack, and the performer places a borrowed dime under one of them. The coin is soon found to have made its way under the other card. The performer then announces that he will cause the coin to appear under either card, as the spectators choose. This may be repeated as often as desired, with the performer showing his hands to be empty every time he turns up a card.

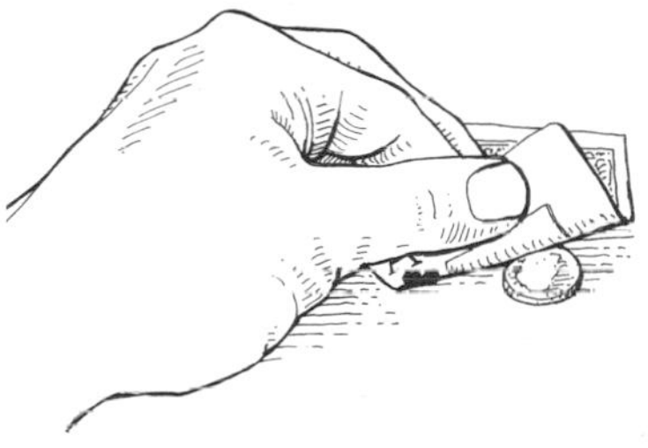

Arching the card to ensure that the dime doesn't stick to it

The secret is this: Have two dimes of your own, each having a little wax on one side. One of these is palmed, the other placed on the servante. Any two cards may be selected. Next, borrow a dime and exchange it unobserved for the waxed one you have palmed. Picking up one of the cards, secretly press one of the waxed coins against it on the underside, thus causing the coin to adhere to the card. Place this card on the table. At the same time, let the left hand, containing the borrowed coin, drop carelessly behind the table, and exchange the borrowed coin for the other waxed one on the servante.

At once, exhibit the coin, place it waxed side up on the table, and place the other card over it, pressing down slightly in the middle over the waxed dime. You may then cause the dime to appear under either card you choose, remembering that if you do not want it to adhere, you may bend the card slightly in turning it up from the table. The dime must of course be secretly exchanged for the borrowed one before returning it, as it would never do to give back a coin having a coating of wax over one side of it!

— The Traveling Coins —

"You all know that money talks," says the smiling wizard. "Now I'll show you how money walks!" So saying, he exhibits eight half-dollars, four of which he places in his right hand and the other four in his left. "Now watch—presto, pass!"

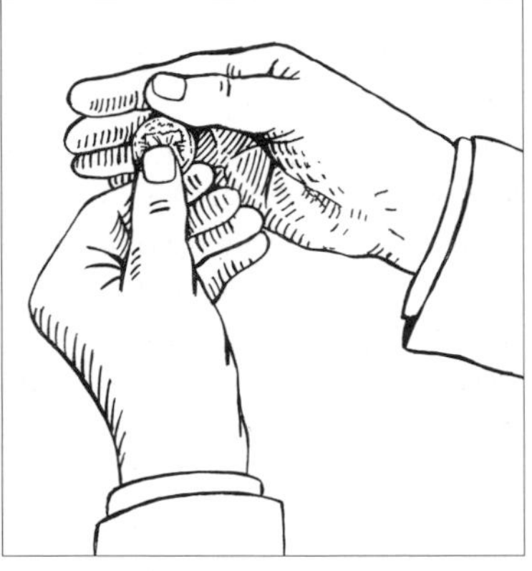

No sooner said than done. The conjurer opens his right hand and drops not four coins, but five. Simultaneously, doing the same with his left hand, he reveals not four half-dollars but three.

This process is repeated three times—and each time, one more coin is found in the right hand and one less in the left, until all four coins have traveled into the right hand.

This trick depends not so much on the manipulative ability of the conjurer as on his address. To perform this surprising feat, you must first have palmed in your left hand a fifty-cent piece—making nine, all told. (Of course, once the presence of this extra coin is suspected, the trick would be ruined.) Now, with the left hand, drop the four coins into the right, one at a time, counting as you do so, "One—two—three." At the word "three," release the palmed coin along with the third coin, so that it drops into the right hand. Then follow that with the fourth. Now it will be seen that the right hand holds five coins. Great care must be taken to do this in as natural a manner as possible. A little practice will be required to drop the two coins from the left hand into the right so that they will "clink" as one. Of course, each time a coin enters the right hand, the fingers must be closed, then opened again to receive the next coin; otherwise, the presence of the extra coin would be detected.

When you pick up the four coins from the table with the left hand, one at a time, count out loud for each coin. Palm the first coin, so that when you drop the five from the right hand, you drop only three from the left, with the fourth one now palmed. Pick up the five other coins with the left hand and drop them into the right hand, singly as before, counting out loud as you do so. With the fourth coin, drop the one palmed, then follow it with the fifth. To all appearances, you have dropped into your right hand six coins. But in reality it now contains seven.

Now, again, pick up the three coins singly with the left hand and, as before, palm the first. Of course, this must be done naturally. Do this a few times without palming, and see just what would be the natural way for you to pick them up. Then practice palming the first coin.

Repeat this process until all four coins have apparently traveled from the left hand to the right. At the conclusion of the trick, you will find that you still have one palmed coin (the ninth, not known to the audience) in the left hand. A most excellent way to get rid of this coin is to pick up all eight exhibited coins with the left hand and let them fall in a shower on the table or into your right hand, assuring the audience that "there is nothing fastened to the coins," and that there really has "been no deception!" You may be sure that no one will notice the extra coin falling with the others.

The entire success of this capital trick depends on the naturalness of the picking up and counting of the coins.

— The Winged Coin —

The effect of this splendid piece of magic is as if you had passed a marked half-dollar from a distance into an uncorked bottle, whose neck was so small that the bottle had to be broken to get the coin out. In appearance, it is as follows: Any gentleman is invited to assist you, and he is seated in a chair at the center of the stage, facing the audience. Take an empty soda-water bottle (one of the round-end variety)

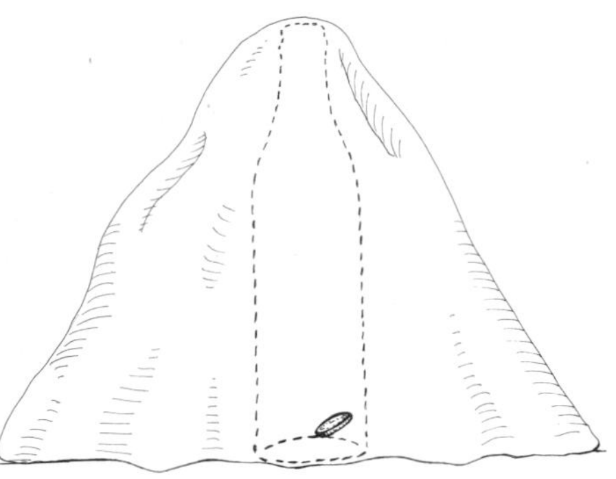
THE PREPARED BOTTLE

and, standing it upright on the volunteer's head, ask him to steady it with his hands so that it does not fall. Now borrow any half-dollar and have it marked by the owner. Taking it in your right hand, make a motion—in full view of your audience—as if throwing it toward the bottle. The sound of a falling coin is heard, and when you ask the gentleman to take down the bottle and shake it, a half-dollar is seen to be within. Take the bottle down among the audience, where it is also seen that the mouth of the bottle is smaller than the coin. Now step up to your table and, taking the hammer, break the bottle over a small box. Picking up the bottom of the bottle, pass it, still containing the coin, to the owner, who identifies his coin.

The secret is this: You have two bottles, one of which is prepared by sawing off the round bottom and placing a half-dollar in the bottle before cementing the bottom on again. On the solid back of the chair is fastened a little wire bottle rack. The prepared bottle has been placed in this beforehand. Beside this little rack is a cloth bag, and as you step up behind the seated subject to place the bottle on his head, rapidly drop the bottle into the bag. With the same motion, bring up to public view the prepared bottle, which you place on the subject's head with the request that he hold it. As the bottom is round, the coin cannot be seen from a distance. The same reason necessitates his holding on to it, else it would tumble over. After vanishing the borrowed coin by palming it, request him to shake the bottle, which he does. The coin is seen to be in it. It is then shown that the neck is too small to admit the half-dollar, after which you hold it over a box containing sawdust and break it. Then pick up the bottom and at the same time substitute the marked coin for the one that was first in it, before passing both bottom and coin to the owner.

— Changing a Button into a Coin —

Put a button in the palm of the left hand, then place a coin between the second and third fingers of the right hand. Keep the right hand facing down and the left hand facing up, so as to conceal the coin and expose the button. With a quick motion, bring the left hand under the right, then stop quickly, and the button will go up the right-hand coat sleeve. Press your hands together, allowing the coin to drop into the left hand. Then expose the palm, now with the coin in it; alternately, rub the hands a little before doing so, saying that you are rubbing a button into a coin.

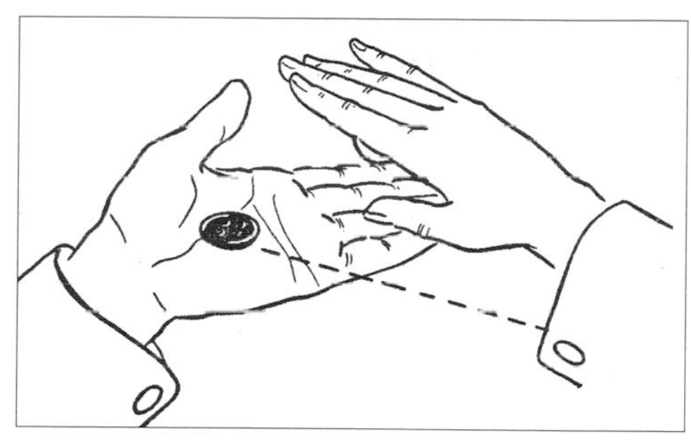

Making the change

— The Forefinger Coin-and-Card Trick —

This is a simple trick that many can do on the first attempt, while others will fail time after time. It is a good trick to spring on a group casually if you have practiced it beforehand. A playing card is balanced on the tip of the forefinger and a penny placed on top, immediately over the finger end, as shown in the sketch. With the right-hand forefinger and thumb, strike the edge of the card sharply. If done properly, the card will fly away, leaving the penny poised on the finger end.

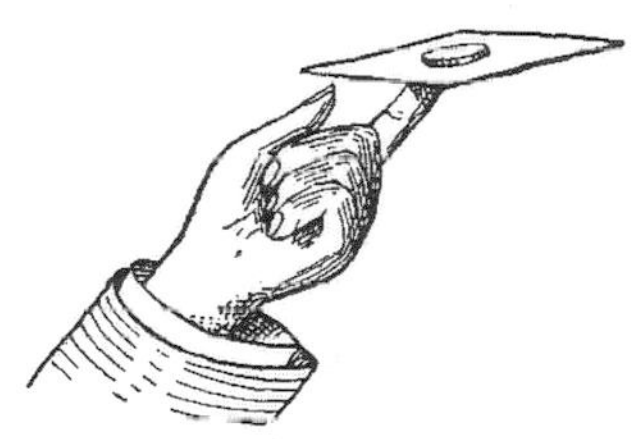

The card will fly away

— The Warm Coin —

A volunteer is chosen to pick one coin from among a dozen in a tray. Then the chosen coin is passed around, so that everyone may see it. This having been done, the one chosen, together with the other eleven, are emptied into a borrowed hat and well shaken up. The performer, who may be blindfolded, puts his hand into the hat and withdraws the selected coin.

The coins kept in a cold metal tray

This is performed as follows: The tray is kept cold prior to the performance. In being handled by the audience, the chosen coin gains a certain warmth while the other eleven remain cold, which can easily be detected by the performer if his hands are at all sensitive.

— The Fifty Cents and Orange Trick —

The following trick will be found to be extremely effective: The magician exhibits a small glass and a pitcher of water. He then asks for the loan of a fifty-cent piece (which may be marked), a handkerchief, and a volunteer from the audience to assist him in the trick. The services of the volunteer having been procured, that person is seated in a chair and given the glass to hold. The performer fills the glass with water, asking his assistant to taste it to see that it is in no way chemically prepared. The conjurer then asks his assistant to hold the marked fifty-cent piece under the handkerchief and over the glass of water. Going to one side of the stage, the performer brings forward two oranges on a plate and allows the audience to choose one of them. He then counts, "One, two, three!" and at the word "three," the assistant is asked to drop the coin he is holding into the water.

With complete silence prevailing, the coin may be heard striking the water and the glass on its downward descent. The performer calls attention to this and says that he will not again approach the glass but will, nevertheless, cause the marked coin to disappear from the tumbler and reappear in the chosen orange. A cap pistol is discharged, the handkerchief is withdrawn from the glass, and the fifty-cent piece is found to have vanished. The water may be poured out, and the tumbler is shown to be empty. On cutting open the orange, the marked coin is found in its center.

The chief secret consists of the use of an ingenious piece of apparatus, of which the audience knows nothing. This is a small disk of glass, the exact size of a fifty-cent piece. In placing the coin under the handkerchief, the performer replaces it with the glass disk, which he had previously palmed. It is this disk that the volunteer holds and that he drops into the glass of water. Being glass, it is naturally invisible when the handkerchief is removed. The tumbler being the exact size (at its base) of a fifty-cent piece, and slightly curved, the water may be poured out and the glass inverted at the conclusion of the trick, without danger of this disk falling out or becoming invisible.

The remainder of the trick is simple. Having possession of the marked fifty-cent piece, the performer secretly introduces it into the center of one of the oranges. The orange has been previously slit open, and the magician advances, asking his audience which orange is preferred. The old dodge is resorted to of forcing the choice (see "Forcing the Card," page 15), so that, no matter which orange is selected, the prepared orange is ultimately the one left for the performance of the trick. All the magician has to do, therefore, is to cut open the orange on the side opposite the slit and break it apart, at which the marked coin will be found in its interior.

A far superior method of loading the coin into the orange, however, is the following: Any orange may be chosen, and it is entirely free from preparation and may be examined by the audience. Only one orange may be used, if desired, and the performer never leaves the stage.

In this case, the coin, when palmed in the left hand, is allowed to drop to the fingertips, and the orange, after being examined, is also picked up in the left hand—thus concealing the coin behind it. The performer cuts the orange into halves with his right hand, turning it around and around. In his hand, as the portion first cut is brought to the back, the fingers work the coin into the slit thus formed—pushing the coin well home while the cutting at the front continues. The result is that when the cutting is complete and the two halves of the orange are separated, there is the half-dollar in the center of the examined orange! This makes a very effective finish to the trick.

— A Simple Coin Trick —

How the poker chip or coin trick is worked

The performer secretly arranges eight coins or eight poker chips in his hand, so that by counting out one chip on the table and the succeeding one under the stack, and so on, he will arrive at alternate heads and tails or alternate colors. The photo and diagram show the proper arrangement. Deal the first chip onto the table, the second one under the stack, the third one onto the table, and so on. "Simple!" That's the cue to hand the stack to the audience.

— The Dropped Quarters —

Take a couple of quarters. Hold the coins between your thumb and forefinger about an inch apart, as shown in the diagram. Now loosen your grip, so that the lower quarter will be released. It is a fairly well-known bit of magic that the released coin will turn over exactly once (half a turn), but can you drop it without making it turn over? A circular snap of the thumb as you release the coin does the trick.

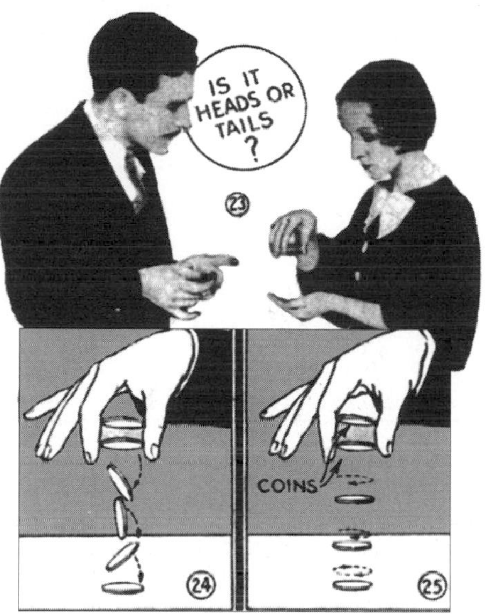

Popular Mechanics

The Boy Mechanic Series

A Note from the Editors

If you've enjoyed *The Boy Magician,* you might like other titles in our *Boy Mechanic* series. To find a complete description of these titles, please visit us at sterlingpublishing.com and type in Popular Mechanics or *Boy Mechanic* in the search field. They are available wherever books are sold.

We'd love to hear what you think about our books. Please contact us directly with any queries and comments by emailing our reader hotline, booklover@hearst.com. We'd love to hear from you.

INDEX

Please note that the projects in this book were created many decades ago when safety standards were more relaxed than they are today. Also, due to differing conditions, tools, and individual skills, the publisher cannot be responsible for any injuries, losses, and/or other damages that may result from the use of the information in this book.

Book design by Barbara Balch

Library of Congress Cataloging-in-Publication Data
The boy magician : 160 amazing tricks & sleights of hand / the editors of Popular mechanics magazine.
p. cm.
Popular mechanics.
Includes index.
ISBN 978-1-58816-754-5
1. Magic tricks. I. Popular mechanics (Chicago, Ill. : 1959) II. Title: Popular mechanics: the boy magician.
GV1547.B7445 2008
793.8--dc22
2008008680

10 9 8 7 6 5 4 3 2 1

Published by Hearst Books
A Division of Sterling Publishing Co., Inc.
387 Park Avenue South, New York, NY 10016

www.popularmechanics.com

For information about custom editions, special sales, premium and corporate purchases, please contact Sterling Special Sales Department at 800-805-5489 or specialsales@sterlingpublishing.com.

Distributed in Canada by Sterling Publishing
c/o Canadian Manda Group, 165 Dufferin Street
Toronto, Ontario, Canada M6K 3H6

Distributed in Australia by Capricorn Link (Australia) Pty. Ltd.
P.O. Box 704, Windsor, NSW 2756 Australia

Manufactured in China

Sterling ISBN 978-1-58816-754-5